EDU
N

THE CLIO MONTESSORI SERIES
VOLUME 5

EDUCATION FOR A
NEW WORLD

Maria Montessori

CLIO PRESS
OXFORD, ENGLAND

Reprinted 1994, 1996, 1997, 1999, 2002, 2005

This edition has been licensed for publication by the Association Montessori Internationale, Amsterdam. *Education For A New World* was first published in 1946.

British Library Cataloguing in Publication Data
Montessori, Maria, *1870–1952*
  Education for a new world.—(The Clio Montessori
  series; 5).
  1. Education. Montessori system
  I. Title
  371.3′92

ISBN 1–85109–095-9

ISBN 1–85109–095-9
ABC-Clio,
26 Beaumont Street
Oxford, OX1 2NP, UK

Typeset by Megaron, Cardiff
Printed and bound in Great Britain by
Latimer Trend & Company Ltd., Plymouth

Cover design by CGS Studios, Cheltenham.

CONTENTS

1

INTRODUCTORY

The purpose of this book is to expound and defend the great powers of the child, and to help teachers gain a new outlook which will change their task from drudgery to joy, from repression to collaboration with nature. Our world has been torn to pieces, and is in need of reconstruction. In this a primary factor is education, the intensifying of which, no less than a return to religion, is generally recommended by the thoughtful. But humanity is not yet ready for the evolution that it desires so ardently, the construction of a peaceful and harmonious society that shall eliminate war. Men are not sufficiently educated to control events, so become their victims. Noble ideas, great sentiments have always found utterance, but wars have not ceased! If education were to continue along the old lines of mere transmission of knowledge, the problem would be insoluble and there would be no hope for the world. Only a scientific enquiry into human personality can lead us to salvation, and we have before us in the child a psychic entity, a social group of immense size, a veritable world-power if rightly used. If salvation and help are to come, it is from the child, for the child is the constructor of man, and so of society. The child is endowed with an inner power which can guide us to a more enlightened future. Education should no longer be mostly imparting of knowledge, but must take a new path, seeking the release of human potentialities. When should such education begin? Our answer is that the greatness of human personality begins at birth, an affirmation full of practical reality, however strikingly mystic.

Already the psychic life in the new-born has aroused great interest, scientists and psychologists having made observations of babes from three hours to five days after birth. The conclusion of these is that the first two years of life are the most important. Observation proves that small children are endowed with special psychic powers, and points to new ways of drawing them out – literally educating – by co-operating with nature. The child's constructive energy, alive and dynamic, has remained unknown for thousands of years, a mine of mental treasure, just as the men who first trod this earth knew nothing of the immense riches that lay hidden in its depths. So far is man from recognizing the riches that lie buried in the psychic world of the child, that from the beginning he has continued to repress those energies and grind them into the dust. Now for the first time a few have come to suspect their existence, a treasure which has never been exploited, more precious than gold, the very soul of man.

Observation of the first two years of life has thrown new light on the laws of psychic construction, which, in childhood, are completely different from the psychology of the adult. So here begins the new path, where it will not be the professor who teaches the child, but the child who teaches the professor.

This may seem absurd, but it becomes clear when the truth emerges that the child has a type of mind that absorbs knowledge, and thus instructs himself. This is easily proved by the child's acquisition of a language – a great intellectual feat. The child of two speaks the language of his parents, though none has taught him. All who have studied this phenomenon agree that at a certain period of life the child begins to use names and words connected with his environment, and soon masters the use of all the irregularities and syntactical constructions that afterwards prove such obstacles to adult students of an alien tongue. So within the child there is a very scrupulous and exacting teacher, who even adheres to a time-table, and at three years produces a being whose acquisitions are already such that it would take an adult sixty years of hard work – psychologists assure us – to achieve as much.

Scientific observation then has established that education is not what the teacher gives; education is a natural process spontaneously carried out by the human individual, and is acquired not by listening to words but by experiment upon the environment. The task of the teacher becomes that of preparing a series of motives of cultural activity, spread over a specially

2

prepared environment, and then refraining from obtrusive interference. Human teachers can only help the great work that is being done, as servants help the master. Doing so, they will be witnesses to the unfolding of the human soul and to the rising of a New Man who will not be the victim of events, but will have the clarity of vision to direct and shape the future of human society.

2

THE DISCOVERY AND DEVELOPMENT OF THE MONTESSORI SYSTEM

If education is to be reformed, it must be based upon the children. No longer is it enough to study great educators of the past, such as Rousseau, Pestalozzi and Froebel; the time for that is over. Further I protest against myself being hailed as the great educator of this century, because what I have done is merely to study the child, to take and express what he has given me, and that is called the Montessori Method. At the most I have been the child's interpreter. My experience is based on forty years beginning with the medical and psychological study of defective children whom I tried to help. These were found to be capable of so much, when approached from the new standpoint of co-operation with their own subconscious minds, that it was decided to extend the experiment to the normal, and Houses of Children were started in some of the poorest districts of Rome for little ones from three years of age. Visitors to these houses were amazed to find children of four years writing and reading, and would ask a child, "Who taught you to write?" The little one would answer, looking up in wonder at the question "Taught? No one has taught me; I did it myself!" The press began to be full of this "spontaneous acquisition of culture," and psychologists were sure that these were specially talented children. For some time I shared that belief, but extended experiments soon proved that all children possessed these powers, and that the most precious years were being wasted, and development was largely thwarted by the fallacious idea that education was possible only after six. Reading and writing are the basic items of culture, for it is impossible to acquire other items without them, and neither is natural to man as the spoken language is. Writing especially is generally considered so arid a task as only to be given to older children. But I gave the letters of the alphabet to four-year-olds, repeating upon normal children experiments first tried on defectives. I had found that just presenting single letters in contrast, day after day, made no impresssion; but when I had caused the forms of the letters to be cut in grooves on wood, and had let them pass their fingers round the grooves, the children recognized the letters immediately. Even defectives, by means of this apparatus, were able after some time to write a little. So I realized that the sense of touch must be a great help to children who had not yet fully developed, and I made simple letters for them to follow round with the tips of their fingers. Quite unexpected phenomena revealed themselves when normal children were given these aids; the letters were presented to the children in the latter half of September, and the children wrote Christmas letters that year! Such rapidity had been undreamt of. The children then began to ask questions about the letters, connecting each with a sound; they seemed to be little absorbing machines for the whole of the alphabet, as if there had been a vacuum in their minds which attracted it. This was surprising, yet it is easy to explain. The letters were a stimulus which illustrated the language already in the mind of the child, and helped him to analyse his own words. When the child possessed only a few letters, if he thought of a name which included sounds other than those he could represent, it was natural for him to ask for them. There was an inner urge for more and more knowlege, and he went about spelling to himself words that he knew how to use in speech. No matter how long and difficult the word, the child could represent it after one dictation by the teacher, by picking out from the prepared compartments of a box the necessary letters. A teacher said a word rapidly in passing, and on return saw that it had been written with the moveable letters. For these mites of four once was enough, though a child of seven or more requires much repetition before he grasps the word correctly. All this was obviously due to that special period of sensitivity; the mind was like soft wax, susceptible at this age to impressions which could not be taken at a later stage, when this special malleability would have disappeared.

As a further result of the inner work going on within the child came the phenomenon of writing. In realizing the formation of the word from its sounds, the child had analysed and reproduced it externally by means of the moveable alphabet. He knew the form of the letter because he had touched it again and again. So writing came suddenly, an explosion like that into speech. When the mechanism has been formed, when it is ripe, the whole of language comes forth, not as usually happens in ordinary schools, first a letter and then a combination of two. If one or two come, then the rest can come; the child knows how to write, and can therefore write the whole language. He now writes continuously, not as a matter of cold obedience to duty, but in enthusiastic obedience to impulse. Those children used everything that they could lay hands on for writing, such as chalk on a road or wall; wherever there was a free space, suitable or not, there would be found writing, even once on a loaf of bread! Their poor illiterate mothers, with no resources of pencil or paper, came for help to satisfy their children's need. We gave help, and the children fell asleep pencil in hand, writing until the last moment of their day.

At first we thought to help them by giving specially ruled paper, with double spacing gradually diminishing in size; but soon we found that these children could write with equal facility in any ruling, and some liked to make their writing as minute as was compatible with legibility. The strangest thing of all was that they wrote beautifully, better than third-year pupils in other schools. Handwritings were all alike, because all had touched the same letters, and so the same form was fixed in their muscular memories.

Now these children knew how to write, but not how to read. This seems at first extraordinary and absurd, but on reflection it was not absurd. Generally children learn first reading and then writing, but our children had first analysed words in their minds, and reproduced them in letters of the alphabet placed side by side, each letter attaching itself to a sound in the language existing in the child's mind. This union between letter and language had taken place during the child's sensitive period, and language had multiplied itself, and was now expressed by means of the hand through writing, instead of only by the lips through speaking. But he could not yet read, and we thought that an obstacle might be the difference between printed letters and the cursive form used in writing. We were thinking of introducing different types of letters to surmount this difficulty when suddenly the children began to read by themselves, and to read any form of print, even the Gothic, which was to be found in calendars. It was five months later than the first attempt to compose with moveable letters, but again an inner urge had been at work in the child, causing him to make an effort to understand the meaning of those unknown letters. He was doing a work similar to that of scientists, who study prehistoric inscriptions in strange languages, and by comparison and close observation derive meanings from unknown signs. A new flame was lit in the heart of the child. Parents complained that they could not take their children for a walk without their stopping before every little shop to puzzle out the signs displayed. At the end of their fifth year, these children could read every book.

There is another side of culture which is not so easily explained as writing: the field of mathematics. We consider mathematics from three points of view:

1. Arithmetic – the science of number.
2. Algebra – the abstract of number.
3. Geometry – the abstract of abstract.

Under the guidance of our experience with children we have given these three together, and at an age almost incredibly early. Uniting the three has been found to be a great help and very effective; it is as if, instead of balancing the subject on a precarious pole, we placed it on three strong feet, which joined together to give great stability. For example, in giving numbers, we group them in geometrical forms, and mathematical material has been built up to give the three subjects almost at the same time. Young children have shown a particular liking, almost a passion, for the study of numbers and their geometrical disposition. Soon after, the abstract of these quantities and their relationships could be made by means of algebra. This also was a matter of great surprise, for at first the child did not show the interest that he had shown in writing. It was easy to say that the child was interested in language, but not in mathematics, which was too dry for him, too abstract! The fact was that we also had prejudices, and had limited mathematics to the four basic rules and within the first ten numbers. It was the child himself who revealed the truth, for when the decimal system was presented to older children, it was the children of five and six who took to it and learnt it with great enthusiasm, which they had not shown for numbers up to a mere ten. To our surprise, the four-year-olds approached this also, to take it in with zest, and now children of three carry out operations involving millions, and we have had to introduce algebra and geometry. If these are introduced as material to be handled, children take to it with delight, and the latest excitement has been to find a child occupied in working out for himself the cube of the trinomial, $(a + b + c)^3$; he had argued within himself that if a and b could be used, why not the other letters of the alphabet, for the child does not like limitations!

This vivid and flashing development does not possess a prehistory, as does language; we cannot trace its beginning and development in the mind before its expression, so we can only deduce that there is a special predisposition at this early age to mathematics. We observe that the acts which arouse in him not only interest, but even enthusiasm, are such as require of him the greatest exactness, and the more complicated the motive, the greater is the enthusiasm of the child. This exactness is seen not only in movement, in the exact manipulation required in some exercise, but also in the study of a flower or an insect. There is a predisposition to exactness and detail, and it may be directed to detail of quantity. Arithmetic is a sort of abstraction, and therefore brings this exactness to the abstract level. The child, starting from the material, passes to the abstract number, and thence to the more abstract stage of algebra, and he works with exactness in all three fields, material, abstract and algebraic, fascinated to be able to realize the play of the units. We are helped to this conclusion by the great philosopher and physicist, Pascal, who was immersed in number and quantity, and who asserted that the human mind has the characteristic of being mathematical, and that the path of progress is along this mental quality. This statement generally arouses hilarity, for the practical experience of ordinary teachers seems to show that of all subjects mathematics is most repugnant to the human mind. Now young children are proving Pascal right! Penetrating deeper into his own conclusion, Pascal said that the whole action of humanity was developed around the environment, and this activity was always within increasingly exact limitations. This exactness could be achieved only by the mind, and proved that the mind had this mathematical quality. The mind of man, as seen in history, is dedicated to the transformation of his environment, and to the interpretation of things around him and phenomena arising out of them. To achieve this it is necessary to be exactly conscious of these things, and to be centred in the field of exactness. Two hundred years ago this quality of exactness was found by Pascal to be a fundamental characteristic of the human mind.

On the important question of fatigue, the child under six has revealed striking facts. In ordinary schools the child soon becomes tired and instruction difficult; hence it has seemed cruel to instruct at an early age, and loving parents want the little ones to do nothing but play and sleep. But there are clear signs that the children themselves get profoundly bored by this programme, and react to it vigorously by all sorts of naughtiness. Experience with our children aged from three to six, and even younger, has shown that not only is there no fatigue in learning at that age, but the children actually become stronger. Not all work brings fatigue; for example, we do much work, as with jaws, teeth and tongue when we eat, and such work results in renewed energy, we feel naturally also a need to exercise our muscles, in order to make them strong. It is the same with children in their mental development. Not only do they seem indefatigable, but by being intellectually active they acquire strength and health. A natural predisposition suits the young child to the reception of culture, but society abandons him mentally at this sensitive period, by its regime of play and sleep. He cannot stop absorbing or stop being active, but if there is nothing to absorb, he has to content himself with toys. Psychologists say that the child must play, for through play he brings perfection to himself. Also they admit that the child absorbs a special environment, and forges the historical link between the past and the future. They conclude that we must observe, without disturbing, the child absorbing the present by playing and living, and not help but abandon him to his own devices. But how can a child in such a complicated world absorb culture if he be left to play with toys and build sand castles? So there is a contradiction in the ideas of these psychologists, who say it is important to communicate with the child in his absorbent stage, and yet he must be left alone, continually to play, as thus he constructs and develops his powers. Play has become exalted as something mystical, and serious and dignified men stand with reverence before a child building sand castles. But it is logical that if there are in this period of three to six natural aptitudes to easy acquisition of culture, we should take advantage of them, and surround the child with things to handle which in themselves convey steps in culture. When we place in his environment certain objects which allow him to imitate human actions around him, and the means to perfect acquisitions already made in the first period, we help him to achieve the complicated culture of today. These are no mere playthings which we give, to be sold along with dolls and tin soldiers. Which do children prefer? When the Montessori material is given, children take to it with vehemence, and to a degree hitherto considered fantastic. These starving minds, which have been thrown into an environment which, alone by themselves, they cannot understand or master, when given means to acquire mastery, hurl themselves on it like hungry lions, devour whatever will help them to survive, and adapt themselves to the civilization that has evolved to date.

Faced with this vision of great power in the child, and of its importance to humanity, we must observe that power minutely, and see in what way we can help it. Instead of placing mystic faith in the play of the child, the faith must be placed in the child himself, and we must do something to create a practical science to use those powers which our intuition has lately come to recognize.

3

PERIODS AND THE NATURE

OF THE ABSORBENT MIND

The new conception takes life at the centre of its own function, and alters all previous ideas about education. No longer may the school be a world apart, or the child carefully protected by isolation from social contacts. For life to receive the right protection, its laws must be sympathetically studied, and psychologists who have observed small children from their first year have announced the discovery that it is in this period that the construction, the building up, of man takes place. Psychically speaking, at birth there is nothing at all – zero! Indeed, not only psychically, for at birth the child is almost paralytic, unable to do anything; and behold him after a while, talking, walking, passing from conquest to conquest until he has built up Man in all his greatness, in all his intelligence! These great powers of the child, which at last have attracted the attention of other scientists than myself, were hitherto hidden under the cloak of motherhood, in the sense that people said that it was the mother who taught her child to talk, walk and speak. But it is not the mother; it is the child himself who spontaneously does these things. What the mother produces is the new-born babe; but it is this babe who produces the man, and does so though the mother may die, or fail to give him the milk needed for his growth. Even what is termed the mother-tongue of the child is not truly derived from the mother, for a child who happens to be born in a land foreign to his parents normally achieves with facility the speech of his environment, though his parents may never master it. So the facility is not inherited; it is due neither to father nor mother, but to the child who, making use of all that he finds around him, shapes himself for the future.

EDUCATION FOR A NEW WORLD

According to modern psychologists who have followed children from birth to university, there are in the course of their development different and distinct periods, corresponding curiously to different phases in the development of the physical body. The changes are so great that certain psychologists, exaggerating in the attempt to render them clear, have expressed themselves thus: "Growth is a succession of births." It seems as if, at a certain period of life, one psychic individual ceases and another is born. The first of these periods goes from birth to six years, and though showing notable differences, throughout its length the type of mind is the same. Two subdivisions are observed in the period, from zero to three years and from three to six, the former showing a mentality that is unapproachable by the adult, who can exercise no influence on it. Then there is the period from three to six, in which the psychic entity begins to become approachable, but only in a special manner. This period is characterized by great transformations that take place in the individual, so that at six years of age the child is commonly thought to be intelligent enough for admission to a school. Following the new line here advocated, he could be usefully admitted to school much earlier, but at six years an epoch is reached, corresponding with changes in the physical body, such as the loss of the first teeth. The period from six to twelve years is one of growth, but no transformations. It is marked normally by serenity and docility. A third period, from twelve to eighteen, is again one of transformations, both psychic and physical. An unconscious recognition has been given to the reality of these periods by official education in all countries, children being admitted to the elementary school at six years, and passing to a higher school at twelve, when a new mental phase begins. During this third period, the character is not steady; there is often indiscipline and some sort of rebellion, but the ordinary school goes its way heedless of these reactions, following its syllabus and punishing rebels. At eighteen may come the University, with its greater intensity of study, but little essential difference of method, for still the student must sit and listen to gain a degree which often proves of doubtful use to him. Physical maturity has been achieved, but all these years of study, all these years of listening, do not form the man of will and judgment. Practical work and experience have to do that, if it still may be done. So even in New York have been seen processions of young intellectuals, bearing banners with the words: "We are without work! We are starving!" A significant indictment of society which has spent so much on their education!

Many a thinker, pondering over the helplessness of the new-born child, has wondered why man, the being endowed with the loftiest intelligence, must have so long and painful an infancy such as no animal suffers. Many have asked what could be taking place in the period of infancy. It was certainly a work of creation, for the individual seemed to start from zero. It is not as though there were in the babe a little voice that later develops, as the kitten develops its imperfect mew, or the calf and young bird merely strengthen in means of self-expression. In the case only of the human being, it is not a question of development, but of creation from nothing. This is the tremendous step the child takes, a step of which the adult is not capable. A type of mind different from that of the adult, endowed with different powers, is necessary for this accomplishment. Indeed this creation of the child is no mean achievement! He creates not only the language, but the organs that enable it to be spoken. He creates every physical movement, every means of intelligent expression.

All this is done not consciously by the will, but with what is called the sub-conscious mind, full of intelligence of a type that is found in all living beings, even in insects, who sometimes seem to be endowed with reason. With this sub-conscious mind the child achieves his wonderful work of creation, through a power of such marvellous sensitivity as resembles to some extent a photographic plate, automatically recording impressions in the minutest detail. The things in his environment seem to awake in the child an intense interest, an enthusiasm that penetrates into his very life. This sub-conscious power can discriminate. Admitted that the child is born with the sense of hearing, so that he hears the human voice, why among the millions of sounds surrounding him does he pick out those only for imitation? It is because human language has made a special impression on the sub-conscious mind, evoking an intensity of feeling, an enthusiasm, able to set in vibration invisible fibres for the reproduction of those sounds, while others cause no such living thrill. So exact is the child's absorption of this language that it forms part of his psychic personality and is called his mother-tongue, to be clearly distinguished from all other languages that he may later acquire with laborious effort. It is a mental chemistry that takes place in the child, producing a chemical transformation. These impressions not only penetrate the mind of the child, they form it; they become incarnated, for the child makes his own "mental flesh" in using the things that are in his environment. We have called this type of mind the "absorbent mind," and it is difficult for us to conceive the magnitude of its powers. If it only could continue! The loss of it is the price we pay for the acquisition of full human consciousness; but it is a heavy price, from God to become man!

4

EMBRYOLOGY

Seeking to penetrate further the mysteries of the absorbent mind, we are led to the investigation of prenatal life and origins, towards which in these days there is a new orientation in all biological studies. Previously the adult specimen of animal or plant life was always the object of consideration, as also the human adult in the study of sociology. Scientists now seem to have taken the opposite direction and, both in the study of human and other types of life, consider the very young and their origin. So the emphasis is on embryology, the life of the germinal cell, the result of two cells which come from adults. The child's life, that which is originated and that which originates, starts from the adult and finishes in the adult; that is the way, the path of life.

Nature furnishes special protection for the young. For instance, the child is born amidst love; his very origin is by love, and once born he is surrounded by the love of father and mother, a love which is not artificial or enforced by reason, such as the sentiment of brotherhood that all thoughtful people are trying to arouse. It is only in the field of the child's life that there can be found the type of love which is the ideal of human morality, the love which inspires self-sacrifice, the dedication of oneself to the service of others. Now this sacrifice that the parents make is something natural, that gives joy, and so is not felt to be a sacrifice; it is life itself! But it is a loftier type of life than the type which finds expression in social competition and the "survival of the fittest." Curiously enough, these two types of life are also to be observed in animals, among which the most ferocious seem to change their natural instincts when they have a family. It is a sort of imposition of the special instincts over the

15

ordinary ones, making timid animals, who possess an instinct of self-preservation to a greater degree than ourselves, entirely change this instinct into one of protection for their young, in reckless disregard for their own safety. So the great French biologist, Fabre, concludes that it is due to this great mother-instinct that the species has survived, and not only to the weapons with which nature has endowed it for the struggle for existence. Are not the young tigers toothless, and the baby birds without feathers? Moreover, it is fascinating to see the revelation of intelligence in even the lower orders of life, wherever it is needed for the protection of the young, not in mere self-defence.

Scientists of the last century thought that there must be in the germinal cell a minute, ready-formed man or woman, that had only afterwards to grow, as in the case of other mammals, and they disputed whether the miniature human being came from the egg-cell of the man or the woman. The invention of the microscope made closer study possible, and the conclusion, very reluctantly accepted, has been that there is nothing pre-existing in the germinal cell. This cell divides itself into two, the two into four, and by multiplication of cells, the being is formed. Embryology has advanced to the point of discovering that there is only a pre-established plan of construction that bears all the marks of reason and intelligence. As a man who builds a house starts by accumulating bricks, so this cell by subdivision accumulates a number of cells, and then builds of them three walls, within which the organs are to be next constructed. The manner of this construction is extraordinary. It begins in one cell, one point, around which the rate of multiplication of cells becomes feverish, whereas elsewhere it continues as before. When this feverish activity ceases, an organ is found to have been built. The discoverer has interpreted the phenomenon in this fashion: these are points of sensitivity around which a construction takes place. These organs develop independently of each other, as though it were the purpose of each to build for itself only, and in their intense activity the cells around each centre become so united, so imbued with what we may call their ideal, that they transform themselves and become different from other cells, assuming a special form according to the organ that is being formed. When the different organs are thus completed independently, something else comes to put them into relation with each other, and when they are so united that one cannot live without the other, the child is born. It is the circulatory system which first joins them, and the nervous system which completes the union. The plan of construction is revealed as based on a point of enthusiasm, from which a creation is achieved, and once the creation of the organs is accomplished, they are destined to join, to unite, for the manifestation of an independent living being. All superior animals follow this plan; there is only one plan of construction in nature.

It seems that the human psyche is constructed on the same lines. It too starts from what appears to be nothing, for in the new-born child also, psychically speaking, there seems to be nothing already built up, and organs are built around a point of sensitivity; here too there is accumulation of material, and this is done by the absorbent mind. After that come points of sensitivity, so intense as to be hardly imaginable to the adult mind, as shown in the acquisition of language. From these points of sensitivity it is not the psyche that is developed, but the organs that the psyche will need. Here also each organ develops independently of the rest; for instance speech, ability to judge distances or to find orientation in an environment, or ability to stand on two legs, and other co-ordinations. Each develops around an interest so acute that it attracts the child towards a set of actions. In each case after the organ has been formed the sensitivity disappears; when all the organs are ready, they unite to form the psychic entity.

It is clear that one cannot understand the construction of the psyche of the child without knowledge of these sensitive periods and their order of occurrence. It is sometimes argued that previous generations had no such knowledge, yet developed into healthy and strong beings; but it should be remembered that we live in a highly artificial civilization, in which the natural instincts with which nature has endowed the mother are largely suppressed or stultified. A simple-living mother still instinctively aids the child in the sensitive period, providing the environment he needs by taking the child everywhere with her, protecting him with her mother-love. Mothers today have largely lost this instinct, and humanity is headed towards degeneration, so it is as important to study the phases of maternal instinct as it is to study the phases of natural development of children, for they were meant to be complementary. Mothers must return to co-operation with nature, or science must find some way of aiding and protecting the psychic development of the child, as it has found ways of aiding and protecting physical development. Maternal love is a force, one of the forces of nature, and it must receive the attention of scientists, so that henceforth mothers may help consciously, as they no longer do instinctively. Education must give the mothers this knowledge, that from birth they may give a conscious protection to the psychic needs of the children, instead of relegating them to hygienically spotless nurseries, to be attended by well-trained nurses, who perfunctorily satisfy their physical needs. It is a fact that such children may even die of what may be called mental starvation, or sheer boredom. This was startlingly demonstrated in a city in Holland where an institution was started to teach poor parents how to keep their children hygienically. Here poor children who had lost their parents were kept under scientifically perfect conditions, well fed and cared for by nurses trained in the latest ideas of hygiene. Illness broke out among these and many died, while the poor children who were brought to the clinic by their parents did not suffer from this illness, and were obviously far healthier than the favoured nurslings of hygiene! So the doctors realized that a vital something was lacking in their institution, and made some changes. Nurses began to imitate the mothers with their own children, taking them up and playing with them, and doing what mothers did who knew nothing of this scientific care, but were guided by natural love and were unable to give them too much protection from social contacts; and the children began to flourish in health and to smile.

5

BEHAVIOURISM

Neither the latest discoveries nor the theories that arise from them can explain fully the mystery of life and its development, but they serve to show and illustrate facts, and allow us to see how growth takes place. One fact that has been established is that the plan of construction is one, and that all types of animal life follow it. The plan can be traced materially in the embryo, can be followed in the study of child psychology, and can also be recognized in society. It is significant that in their earlier stages animal embryos are all alike, whether of man, rabbit or lizard. To realize themselves, vertebrates have to pass through the same phases; but when the embryonic development is completed, the difference is immense. It may be asserted with the same certainty that the new-born babe is a psychic embryo, so that at birth all children are alike, and need the same treatment or education during the stage of embryonic growth, of mental incarnation. No matter what type of man may result from the work of the child, a world-genius or a labourer, saint or criminal, each must pass through these phases of incarnation. Accordingly education in the first years of life must be alike for all, and must be dictated by nature herself, who has infused certain needs into the growing being. It is true that differences afterwards arise in individuals, but we neither cause those differences nor are we even able to provoke them. There is an inner individuality, an ego, which develops spontaneously, independently of us, and we can only help him who is potentially a genius, a general or an artist, to realize himself, and remove obstacles in his path of growth towards realization. We have established the fact of the existence of points of sensitivity, around which organs are formed, and then of the coming of the two systems, circulatory and nervous, to conduct and unite. But science cannot explain the further fact of the coming into existence of a living being, free and independent, different from all others, having its own character.

In 1930 a biological discovery was made in Philadelphia which entirely contradicted current theories. It was found that the visual nerve centre in the brain was formed before the optic nerve, and long before the eye. The conclusion was that in animals the psychic form precedes the physical, and it follows that the instincts of each animal, and the natural habits of each, are fixed before the part which will express them is formed. If this psychic part pre-exists, it means that the physical part finishes its own construction, moulding itself to the requirements of the psyche, of the instincts; the organs and the limbs of animals, whatsoever their species, are such as are best suited to express these instincts. The new theory is know as Behaviourism, and it is contrary to the old belief that animals assumed habits in order to adapt themselves to environment. It was thought that the will of the adult provoked the necessary modifications of bodily structure in the struggle for survival, and that gradually, through successive generations, perfect adaptation was achieved. The new theory does not deny all of this, but puts, as the centre of all, the instinctive habits or behaviour of the animal. It can succeed in its efforts towards adaptation only if these be expended within the limits of its own behaviour. An example may be found in the case of the cow, a powerful creature, strong and well built. Its evolution can be traced in the geological history of the world. It makes its appearance when the earth is already well supplied with vegetation, and one asks why this animal has chosen to feed only on grass, the most indigestible food that can be found, so requiring the development of four stomachs. If the question were one only of survival, it would have been easier to eat something else, of which there was abundance. Millions of years have elapsed since then, but we still see cows, under natural conditions, eating only grass. Observing closely, one sees the cow cropping the grass close to the roots, but never uprooting the plant; it is as if they knew that grass needs to be cut near the roots for development of underground stems, or it soon comes to fruition and dies. Again, grass is found to be of tremendous importance for the preservation of other vegetable forms of life, because grass knits together the loose grains of sand and soil which otherwise the wind would carry away. Not only does it stabilize the ground, but it also fertilizes it, preparing the ground for other vegetation; such is the importance of grass in nature's economy. But two things, beside cutting, are necessary to its upkeep; one is manure, the other rolling or pressure under a heavy weight. What agricultural machine can perform these three tasks better than the cow does? This marvellous machine moreover provides milk, besides assisting the growth of grass and the whole upkeep of earth. So the behaviour of the cow seems designed for the purposes of nature, just as that of crows and vultures is designed for efficient service in another department, that of scavenging.

These examples concern the animals' choice of food, and the conclusion justified from hundreds of such cases would be that animals do not eat merely to satisfy themselves, but to fulfil a mission prescribed to them by their behaviour, in the interests of the harmony of creation, which is achieved by the collaboration of all beings, animate and inanimate. There are other creatures which eat in such inordinate measure that it cannot be merely for the upkeep of life. They do not eat to keep alive, but they keep alive in order to eat! An instance is the earthworm, which eats daily a quantity of earth calculated as two hundred times the volume of its own body. It was Darwin who first said that without the worms the earth would be less productive.

The bees' work in the fertilization of flowers is another familiar instance, and we begin to see in this behaviourism that animals sacrifice themselves for the sake of other types of life, instead of eating merely for their own continued existence. Similarly, in the ocean there are uni-cellular organisms which act as filters, ridding the water of certain poisonous salts, and in the pursuit of this function they drink such enormous quantities in proportion to their size as to be equivalent to a man's consumption of a gallon per second for life! The purpose which places the animals in relation to the earth and its upkeep would never enter the consciousness of the animals, yet upon their tasks depend higher forms of life, the very surface of the earth, the purity of air and of water.

All this makes it clear that there is a pre-established plan, for the fulfilment of which organs are formed, and the purpose of life is to obey the occult command which harmonizes all and creates an ever better world. The world was not created for us to enjoy, but we are created in order to evolve the cosmos.

Studying human kind, and comparing it with other animal types, we find some differences, and the main one is that humanity has not had allotted to it a special kind of movement, or a special kind of residence. Of all animals man is most capable of adapting himself to any climate, tropical or arctic, desert or jungle; man alone is free to go wherever he likes. Man also is capable of the most varied movements, and can do things with his hands which no other animal has ever been able to do. There seem to be no limits in man's behaviour; he is free. Mankind has the most varied language; in movements he can walk, run, jump and crawl; he is capable of artificial movements in dancing, and can swim like a fish. In the child, however, none of these abilities are present at birth; each has to be conquered by the human being during early childhood. He who is born without power of movement, almost paralysed, can learn by means of exercise to walk, run and climb like other animals, but it must be by his own effort. The child not only acquires all the human faculties, far more varied than those of other animals, but also has to adapt the being that he constructs to the climatic and other conditions in which he will have to live, and to the claims of a civilization growing ever more complicated. If men were fixed in their behaviour as animals are, they would not be able to adapt themselves to new conditions, changing for each generation. The task of adapting seems to be set by nature only for childhood's accomplishment; the adult is not adaptable. The adult looks on his own land as the most desirable spot on earth, whatever its drawbacks, and can never completely master the sounds of a foreign language, though they may be far simpler than his own, which he acquired with ease in infancy. Adults may admire an environment and remember it, but the child can absorb it unconsciously and form with it part of his psyche; he thus incarnates in himself the things that he sees and hears, such as language, and real transformations take place. This kind of memory is called by the psychologists the Mneme, and its task is to construct for the individual a behaviour suited to the time and place, but also to the mentality of its society. Adults find themselves with sentiments and prejudices, especially religious ones, which perhaps their reason may reject; but they can never quite get rid of them, as they are part of themselves, truly "in their blood," as the saying goes.

It follows that, if we wish to alter the habits and customs of a country, or if we wish to accentuate more vigorously the characteristics of a people, we must take as our instrument the child, for very little can be done in this direction by acting upon adults. To change a generation or nation, to influence it towards either good or ill, to re-awaken religion or add culture, we must look to the child, who is omnipotent. The truth of this has been demonstrated of late by Nazis and Fascists, who changed the character of whole peoples by working on children.

6

EDUCATION FROM BIRTH

The new-born child is far from full development; even physically he is incomplete. The feet destined to walk the earth, and perhaps invade the whole world, are yet without bones, cartilaginous; the cranium, that encloses the brain and should be its strong defence, has only a few of its bones developed. More important still, the nerves are not completed, so that there is a lack of central direction and of unification between the organs, and therefore no movement, though the new-born of other creatures have power to move, and walk almost at once. In fact the child must be considered as possessing an embryonic life that extends before and after birth. This life is interrupted by a great event, the adventure of birth, by which he plunges into a new environment. The change in itself is terrific, as though one went from the earth to the moon. But this is not all; in order to take the great step the child must undergo a tremendous physical effort. When a child is born, people generally think only about the mother and her difficulties, but the child passes through a still greater trial, especially when it is considered that the child is not even complete, though endowed with a psychic life. He has not the psychic faculties because he has first to create them; so this psychic embryo, which even physically is not complete, must create its own faculties.

This being which is born powerless, motionless, must be endowed with a behaviour that leads it towards movement. Those instincts which in other animals seem to awaken at birth, as soon as the animal comes into contact with its environment, in man must be built by the psychic embryo at the same time as it builds the faculties to which the movements correspond. While this goes on, the physical part of the embryo is finishing its development, the nerves becoming unified and the cranium ossified.

Chickens, on coming out of eggs, only wait for the mother-hen to show them how to pick up food, and they immediately start to behave like other chickens. This is their present habit, it was the same in previous generations, and it is to be expected that it will always be so. But man must develop his psyche first, and this must accord with the environment and changing conditions in an evolving human society; so nature has taken the precaution of keeping the body inert while both skeleton and nervous system give priority to the development of intelligence. If psychic life is to incarnate the environment, the intelligence must first observe and study it, must in fact gather up a great number of impressions from it, just as the physical embryo begins by accumulating cells, before starting to use them to build its special organs.

So the first period of life has been fixed for the storing of impressions from the environment, and is therefore the period of the greatest psychic activity; it is the activity of absorbing everything that there is in the environment. In the second year the physical being nears completion, and movement begins to become determined. Formerly it was thought that the small child had no psychic life, whereas now we realize that the only part of him which is active during the first year is the brain! The chief characteristic of the human babe is intelligence, unlike the other animals who only need to awaken the instincts towards their behaviour. The human child's intelligence has to take in the present of an evolving life which goes back hundreds of thousands of years in its civilization, and which has stretching before it a future of hundreds of thousands of millions of years; a present that has no limit either in the past or the future, and that is never for a moment the same. Its aspects are infinite, whereas for the others there is but one aspect which is always fixed. Certainly this psyche of man must begin in some mysterious fashion, and it is proved to have begun before birth, because in the mind of the new-born we find powers so strong that they have the possibility of creating any faculties, of adapting man to any condition.

Psychologists of today are struck by what they call "the difficult adventure of birth," and conclude that the child must undergo a great shock of fright. One of the scientific terms used in psychology is "birth terror"; it is not a conscious terror, but undoubtedly the new-born can feel fright, as when lowered too quickly into a bath, or when exposed to strong light and strange handling. Nature gives a simple mother the instinct of keeping the child close to her own body; she is not left with too much energy, so that, in keeping quiet for her own sake, she gives the needed quiet to the child, warming it with her own warmth and protecting it from many impressions. Mother cats hide their young in some dark hole, and jealously guard them from alien touch, but most human mothers have largely lost their natural instinct; as soon as the child is born, somebody comes to wash and dress it, taking it to the light to see the colour of the eyes, from ignorance exposing it to further shock and fright. The consequence of such "birth terror" is recognized today in faults of character assumed by the child in later development; a psychic transformation takes place, and, instead of being normal, the child pursues a wrong path. Faults so caused have been included in the term "psychic regressions," and they are characterized by a shrinking from life, as if these beings remain attached to something which existed before birth, feeling repulsion to the world. Long hours of sleep in the new-born are considered normal but it can be too long to be normal, when it shows regression. Another sign is the habit of waking up crying, and frequency of nightmares; another the over-close attachment to someone, generally the mother, as from fear to be left alone. Such a child is of the type who cries easily, who requires always someone to help him, who will remain lazy, depressed, timid. It is evident that such beings are inferior to others in the struggle for life; it will not be their lot to have joy, courage and normal happiness. This is the terrible answer of the sub-conscious psyche. We forget with our conscious memory, but the impressions engraved upon the mneme remain as characteristics of the individual. Therein lies a great danger to humanity. The child who is not properly cared for takes vengeance on society by forming a weak individual, an obstacle to the progress of civilization.

In contrast to these regressives, the normal child shows tendencies which are strongly set towards independence. The development is by conquest of ever greater independence, overcoming every obstacle on the way. The vital force which provides this urge is called Horme, and is comparable to the force of will in the adult, though the latter is far smaller and limited to the individual, while the horme belongs to life in general, a divine force working for evolution. In the normally growing child it is manifest in enthusiasm, happiness, the "joy of life." At birth he frees himself from a prison, the mother's body, and achieves independence of the functions of the mother; he is endowed with the urge to face and conquer the environment, but for this the environment must be attractive to him. What he feels may not inappropriately be called a love for his environment. The first organs which begin to function are the sensory organs, and the normal child takes in everything, not yet distinguishing sound from sound, object from object; first it takes the world, and then analyses it.

At the age of six months certain phenomena present themselves; these are signposts of normal growth. There are physical changes, the stomach beginning to secrete an acid necessary for digestion, and the first tooth makes its appearance. This is a great step to independence. It is also about this time that he begins to utter the first syllable, the first stone laid in the great building which will develop into a language. Soon he can express himself, and has not to depend on others to guess his needs; truly, a great conquest towards independence. Some time after this achievement, at the age of one year, the child begins to walk, thus freeing himself from a second prison. By these successive steps, man becomes free but it is not as yet a matter of will; independence is a gift of nature, leading him to freedom.

The conquest of walking is a very important one, highly complex, and yet made in the first year of life, together with the other conquests of language and orientation. Inferior animals walk as soon as they are born, but the construction of man is more refined and needs more time. The power to stand on two legs and to walk erect depends on the development of the part of the brain called the cerebellum, which begins very rapid growth at six months, and continues to develop rapidly until the child is fourteen or fifteen months old. In exact accordance with this growth the child sits up at six months, starts to crawl at nine months, stands at ten and walks between twelve and thirteen months, while at fifteen months he walks with security. A second factor in this conquest of walking is the completion of certain spinal nerves, through which messages from the cerebellum pass to the muscles; and yet a third is the completion of the bony structure of the feet, and of the cranium, so that the brain may be protected from injury in a fall.

No education can teach a child to walk before its time; here nature herself commands and must be obeyed. Further, it is futile to try to keep the child still who has started to walk and run, because nature directs that any developed organ must be put to use. Similarly, as soon as language appears the child begins to chatter, and one of the most difficult things is to make him stop talking. If the child were not to talk and to walk, there would be an arrest in his development, so he must be left free to function, to use his independence. Psychologists say that behaviour is affirmed in each individual by experiment carried out on the environment, and therefore the first task of education is to furnish an environment which will permit and aid the child to develop the functions given him by nature. This is not a question of merely pleasing the child, but of co-operation with a command of nature.

Observation of the child shows that normally he has the desire to act independently; he wants to carry things, to dress and undress alone, to feed himself, and it is not by adult suggestion that he tries to do these things. On the contrary, his urge is so strong that our efforts are usually spent in trying to restrain him; but when we do this, we are fighting nature, not the will of the child. Next he will show the tendency to develop his mind through his own experience, and so begin to seek out the reason of things. This is no theory, but clear natural fact, revealed and confirmed by observation. We say that society must render the freedom of the child complete, must assure his independence, but this ideal of freedom and independence is not to be confused with the vague conceptions of adults in using those words. In reality most people have a very miserable idea of what freedom means. Nature gives life by giving freedom and independence, but with it gives laws determined in accordance with the time and its special needs. Nature makes freedom a law of life – the choice only to be free or to die. Nature now offers us help and aid for the interpretation of our social life through observation of the child, who shows us reality. Independence is revealed as not a static thing but a continuous conquest, the acquisition by untiring work not only of freedom, but of strength and self-perfection. In giving freedom and independence to the child, we free a worker who is impelled to act and who cannot live except by his activity, because this is the form of existence of all living beings. Life is activity, and it is only through activity that perfection of life can be sought and found. Some social aspirations that have come to us through the experience of past generations, presenting an ideal of fewer working hours, of other people working for us, are natural characteristics of a degenerate child who shuns life.

A special problem of education is how to help these degenerate children, how to cure regressions which retard or cause deviations from normal development. Since such a child has no love of environment and feels obstacles to his conquest of it too difficult to surmount, the first need is to diminish the obstacles, and then to give attraction to the environment. Then the child must be given pleasant activity, something of interest to do, inviting him to carry out further experiments. Gradually the child may be brought, from the desire to laze, to interest in something which awakens a desire for work, from sluggishness to activity, from that state of fright which often translates itself into an attachment so strong as to resist any parting, to a freedom of joy and the conquest of life.

Certain principles may now be enunciated for education in the first two years of a child's life. The baby should remain as much as possible with the mother directly after birth, and the environment must not present obstacles to his adaptation; such obstacles are change of temperature from that to which he has been accustomed before birth, too much light and too much noise, for he has come from a place of perfect silence and darkness. The child must be carefully handled and moved, not lowered suddenly to be plunged into a bath, and rapidly and roughly dressed – roughly in the sense that any handling of a new-born child is rough because he is so exquisitely delicate, psychically as well as physically. It is best of all if the newborn child is not dressed, but rather kept in a room sufficiently heated and free from draughts, and carried on a soft mattress, so that he remains in a position similar to the prenatal one. The tendency today is to give the babe the same care and consideration – only yet more refined and perfect – as is given to badly wounded men. Besides hygienic care and protection, the mother and child should be looked on as two organs of one body, still vitally connected by animal magnetism; they need seclusion for some time and very careful consideration in every way. Relatives and friends should not kiss and fondle the infant, nor nurses remove him from his mother's side.

Once this first stage is past, the child adapts himself easily to the world he has entered, and begins to travel on the path of independence. His first conquest is the use of the senses, a purely psychic activity, for his body as yet is inert. The child's eyes are very active: he not only receives impressions through them, but seeks them, like an active research worker. Unlike the lower animals who are limited in their observation, and are attracted to certain things only under the guidance of their behaviour, he has no limits, but takes in the whole environment, incorporating it in his psyche. He wants the world – all of it that is around him – to build up his adaptation to it. It is a mistake to seclude the child in a nursery, a sort of prison, with a nurse for sole companion, and make him sleep as much as possible, like an invalid. The nurse does not speak much to him, because it is hygienic to keep the mouth covered, so how can the child learn the language? Besides, the nurse belongs to a different social environment from that of the child, so that he cannot absorb from her the language he will need. Rich children in the most highly civilized countries are the most ill-used in this respect, seeing little of their mother or her friends, left to inhumanly competent nurses, protected in perambulators by hoods from sun and cold, so unable to feast their eyes on anything more interesting than a nurse's face. They either become apathetic and dull, or react by fits of crying and temper, because they suffer from mental starvation and are at least mentally under-nourished. Happier is the child who goes everywhere with his mother, in streets and market, in trams and buses, listening and looking, storing up impressions of intense interest, and secure all the time in the care of his natural protector.

7

THE MYSTERY OF LANGUAGE

A language is the expression of agreement among a group of men, and can be understood only by those who have agreed that special sounds shall represent special ideas. Other groups have other sounds to represent the same ideas and things, so language becomes a wall that separates group from group, while uniting members of the same group. It is the instrument of thinking together, and has become ever more complicated as man's thought grew in complexity. The sounds used to compose words are few, but they can unite in many ways to make words, and these words can be grouped in many ways to form a sentence for the expression of a thought. There is nothing more mysterious than the truth that for any achievement men must come together and agree, and for this agreement they must use language, the most abstract of things, a sort of super-intelligence.

There have been languages that became so complicated and rigidly formal that they died, derivative tongues taking their place in common use; but, however difficult we may now find it to acquire a thorough knowledge of classical Latin, the slaves of imperial Rome must have spoken it, and peasants as they laboured in the fields, though none had taught them. Three-year-old children must also have found it easy to speak and understand. This mystery today has aroused curiosity, and psychologists, considering the development of language in children, emphasize that it is developed, not taught! Language comes naturally, as a spontaneous creation, and to a striking degree its development follows definite laws, and in certain epochs reaches certain heights; moreover this is true for all children, whether the language of their race be simple or complex. There is a period for all children when only syllables are spoken; then another when words are spoken of more than one syllable; ultimately the whole syntax and grammar seem to be grasped, gender and number, case, tense and mood. The child who has a cultured environment has learnt to use its language correctly in the same time as the poor African child has learnt his few words. The sounds which compose words are made by the use of certain bodily mechanisms, as the tongue, throat and nose, and certain muscles of the cheek. The construction of this mechanism is found to be perfect only for speaking the mother-tongue; of a foreign tongue, adults cannot even hear all the sounds, much less make them to perfection. Only the child under three can construct the mechanism of language, and he can speak any number of languages, if they are in his environment at birth. He begins this work in the darkness of the sub-conscious mind, and here it develops and fixes itself permanently. Changes take place in the depths not readily accessible to adult observation; but some external manifestations may be seen and checked, and these are significant and clear, common to all humanity. One conclusion is that the sounds of any language keep their purity age after age, and another that complexities are taken in by the child's sub-conscious mind as easily as simplicities. No child becomes tired of learning to speak; his mechanism has supplied language in its wholeness, much as the mechanism of a camera film acts with the same ease in photographing ten or more people as in producing the likeness of one. The film takes the picture in a fraction of a second, but it would take time and effort to draw the likeness of one man, and ten times as much to draw ten.

A further interesting analogy is that the photograph is taken and developed in darkness; only when it is fixed can it be brought to the light, and then it is unalterable. So it is with the human mechanism for language in the child: it begins deep in the darkness of the sub-conscious, is developed and fixed there, and only then is it seen openly.

Observations patiently carried out and accurately recorded day by day after birth have established certain facts which are like milestones. There is a mysterious inner development which is very great, while the corresponding outer sign of it is very little, showing great disproportion between the inner activity and its manifestation. Progress is found to be not regular and graphically linear, but in jerks, so that between the conquest of syllables and that of words months elapse, in which no progress seems to have been made. Again the child seems at a standstill with a few words for a long time, but in the inner life there is a continuous and great progress, resulting suddenly in what the psychologists call an explosive phenomenon. At the same period of life in each child comes suddenly a cataract of words, all pronounced perfectly. Within three months the children use with ease idioms and lingual idiosyncrasies, and all this happens at the end of the second year for the normal child of any race. These phenomena continue after age two, with mastery of the use of complex sentences, tenses and moods of verbs and syntactical difficulties appearing in the same explosive way in turn, till the expression of the language is complete. Only then is this treasure which has been prepared by the sub-conscious handed over to consciousness, and the child makes full use of his new power, chattering incessantly and irrepressibly.

Two-and-a-half years seems to be the border line of intelligence, when man is formed. After that, development is no longer explosive, but the child enriches his vocabulary if he is in a cultured environment, and, even in less favourable circumstances, enlarges it. Scientific observers in Belgium noted the fact that, whereas at two-and-a-half the child knew only two hundred words, at five he new and used thousands – and all without a teacher. After learning all this by himself, he is admitted to a school and taught the alphabet!

Further facts concerning the mechanisms of language need consideration. In the cortex of the brain are two centres, one being aural, for heard language, the other motor, for the production of language. The receptive or hearing centre is related to that mysterious part of the psyche in which language is sub-consciously developed, and with the ear. This organ of hearing is completed before birth, and is a sort of harp, with sixty-four strings, placed in gradation of length in the form of a shell, to economize space. Not all the sounds of the universe can be taken in by the ear, since there are but sixty-four strings, but quite complex music can be played on it; a language, with all its delicate variations of tone and accent can be transmitted by it. The curious thing is that, according to the psychologist, the sense most slow to develop is hearing; all sorts of noises can be made around the child without any reaction. But this is because those centres in the brain are designed for language, and this whole mechanism responds only to the spoken word, so that in due time the mechanism of movement will be produced, to reproduce the same sounds that it received. If this special isolation of these centres had not taken place, and they had been left free to receive any sound, the child born on a farm would have been impressed by the predominant sounds of farm life, and would bleat, grunt and cackle, and the child born close to a railway would reproduce the whistling and puffing of trains. It is because nature has built and prepared these centres specially for human language that man can speak. There have been authenticated cases of wolf-children, human babies who, for one reason or another, have been abandoned in the jungle, and by some wonderful means have managed to live. These children, although they have had round them all kinds of animal and bird sounds, have remained entirely dumb; they had heard no human speech which alone could provoke the mechanism of spoken language. Humanity is distinguished by this power, not to possess language, but to possess the mechanism for creating a language. In those mysterious places of the brain is a god, a sleeping self, who seems to be awakened by the music of the human voice, a divine call, setting fibres in vibration. Every human group loves music, creates its own music and its own language, and responds to its own music with movements of the body; this music attaches itself to words, but the words have no sense in themselves until human agreement put the meaning to them.

At four months – some say even earlier – the child perceives that this mysterious music, which surrounds him and couches him so deeply, comes from a human mouth; the lips move to produce it. See with what intensity a baby watches the lips. Consciousness is already taking part in the work, though movement has been unconsciously prepared; now comes conscious interest, to enliven and make a series of keen, alert researches. Having thus closely observed for two months, the baby produces his own sounds; suddenly he can say "Da-da-da," or "Ma-ma-ma," articulate syllables. By the end of ten months he has discovered that speech is not just music to be imitated as closely as possible, but that there is purpose in the sounds addressed to him. So by the end of the first year two things have happened: in the depths of the unconscious he has understood, and in the heights of consciousness he has created language, though as yet only babbling, just repeating sounds and their combinations. Then he utters his first intentional words, still babbling, but with conscious meaning. Here a great struggle arises within the child, of the consciousness against its mechanism. It is an epoch when the intelligence has many ideas, and he knows people could understand, if only he had language for their expression; it is the first disappointment of life and it drives him to school, in his sub-conscious, spurring him to learn. It is the conscious impulse that makes this hurried acquisition of language, and his inner teacher makes him go to the adults who are talking to each other, not to him. The impulse forces him to take the language in its correct form, and through ignorance of his real needs most adults talk only "baby language" to him, giving him no help. We must realize that the child has knowledge, and we can talk to him grammatically and aid him in analysing sentences. The child of one or two years may have something to tell that he feels to be very necessary, and be unable to find the word he wants, so he becomes agitated, even enraged, and it is all put down to "original sin." Poor little man who is working towards independence! To be so misunderstood! Rage is the only expression open to him if the right means are lacking.

At about one-and-a-half years of age the child has grasped the fact that each object has a name, so that, among the words that he has learnt, he can now pick out sounds, especially concrete ones. It is important to him, because he can now ask for what he wants, and he crowds into one word a whole phrase, so that the mother or teacher should give much sympathetic study to interpreting him, bringing calm to a tormented soul. To illustrate by an example, a Spanish baby was being carried by his mother on the occasion of a picnic, when summer heat led the mother to take off her coat and carry it over her arm. Immediately the child began to get agitated, and when no one understood his utterance of "To palda," took to screaming violently. At my suggestion the mother put on her coat, and the child was at once appeased, and crowed in happiness. The cryptic words had been abbreviations of "Palto" the Spanish for "overcoat," and "Espalda," which is "shoulders." So in reality the child's sense of order had been outraged by the wrong position of the coat on his mother's arm. Such disorder had been more than he could bear.

Another example reveals how much a child of one-and-a-half years can understand a whole conversation. Some five people were discussing the value of a child's story, and ended their talk with the remark, "It all ends happily." With this conclusion the baby was in decided disagreement, and he began to cry: "Lola, Lola!" It was thought that the little one wanted his nurse, and was calling her by name but that did not help, and he only became more distressed and angry, till at last he managed to get hold of the book, and show on the back cover a picture of the child crying. How could it end happily if it left a crying child? The word "Lola" was an attempt at the Spanish "llora," and it became clear that the child had followed the whole conversation intelligently.

Largely owing to adult misunderstanding, agitation forms an integral part of the life of children. The fact is that there is an inner wealth which tries to find expression, and can only do so amid great difficulties, both of the environment and of the child's own limitations. Certain children are stronger than others, and some have a more favourable environment, and these go straight to independence – the path of normal development – without regressions. It is the same with the conquest of language – a greater independence – which ends in freedom of expression, but has also its parallel dangers of regression. The effect of obstacles at this time will remain permanently, since all impressions at this epoch are eternally registered. Adults often suffer from difficulties in speaking, ranging from hesitation and want of courage to stammering, and these defects had their birth when the mechanisms of speech were being organized. These regressions happen because of the sensitivity of the child; just as he is sensitive to what aids him to produce, so also is he sensitive to obstacles that are too strong for him, and such sensitivity will remain with him for the rest of his life as a defect. Any form of violence, in speech or action, does irreparable harm to the child, and another deviated sensitivity is due to the calm but determined effort of some adult to restrain outer manifestations of children. Mothers who can afford what is called a well-trained nurse for their children should specially beware of this tendency in her to say "Don't do this," "You mustn't do that," with the result that some form of impediment of speech is very common among aristocrats, who do not lack physical courage, but hesitate or stammer painfully in their speech.

Many a senseless fear and nervous habit to be found in adults is now traced back to some violence to the child's sensitivity; therefore it is important for humanity that this epoch of child life should be closely studied. The teacher should embark on this path of discovery, trying to penetrate the mind of the child, as the psychoanalyst penetrates the unconscious of the adult. An interpreter is needed for the child and his language, and my own experience in this capacity is that children run eagerly to their interpreter, realizing that here they can find help. Such eagerness is quite other than the casual affection returned by a child who is petted and caressed; the interpreter is to the child a great hope, opening to him a door which the world has closed. Such a helper is taken into the closest relationship, more than affection, because he gives help and not mere consolation.

8

MOVEMENT AND ITS PART

IN EDUCATION

Movement is the conclusion and purpose of the nervous system; without it there can be no individual. The nervous system, along with brain, senses, nerves and muscles, puts man into relationship with the world, unlike the other organized systems of the body, which are exclusively at the service of the physical individual, and so are called organs of the vegetative life. The vegetative systems help man to enjoy bodily purity and health, but the nervous system has a higher purpose than an analogous purity and uplift of mind. The behaviour of animals is not merely directed to beauty and grace in movement, but has a deeper purpose, to aid the universal economy of nature; so also has man a purpose, not just to be purer and finer than others, but to use his spiritual riches, his aesthetic greatness, in the service of others. Powers must be expressed, and so complete the cycle of relationship. This point of view must be taken into account not only in the practice of life, but in education. If we have a brain, senses and organs of movement, these must function, and if every part is not exercised, we cannot even be sure of understanding them. Movement is the last part that completes the cycle of thought, and spiritual uplift is attained through action or work. People ordinarily think that the muscles have to be used to stay healthy, so in order to move they play tennis, or go for a walk to promote better digestion and sleep forsooth! This mistake has crept into education, and it is as absurd as it would be to make a great prince the servant of a shepherd. The princely muscular system has become a handle to turn for the better functioning of the vegetative systems. This is a great mistake; physical life is entirely separated from mental life so games have to be put into the curriculum that the child may develop physically as well as mentally. It is true that mental life has nothing to do with physical pastimes, but we cannot separate what nature has put together. By considering physical life on the one side and mental on the other we break the cycle of relation, and the actions of man remain generally separated from the brain. Man's actions are directed to aid eating and breathing, whereas movement should be the servant of the whole life, and of the spiritual economy of the world.

It is fundamental that the actions of man should be connected at the centre – the brain – and put in their place. Mind and movement are two parts of a single cycle, and movement is the superior expression. Otherwise man develops as a mass of muscles without brain; something is out of place, as with a broken bone, incapacitating the limb. It is essential for our new education that mental development be connected with movement and dependent on it. Without movement there is no progress and no mental health. The truth of this needs no formal demonstration and proof; conviction comes by watching nature and observing her facts, and specially watching the development of the child. Scientific observation shows that intelligence is developed through movement; experiments in all parts of the world have confirmed that movement helps psychic development, and that development in turn expresses itself in further movement, so there is a cycle, which must be completed, because mind and movement belong to the same unity. The senses also help; any deficiency in them causes the child to be less intelligent.

It is logical that movement should be a higher expression of the psyche, for those muscles which depend on the brain are called voluntary muscles, being moved by the will of the individual, and will is that primal energy without which psychic life cannnot exist. The muscles form the greater part of the body, giving it form. They are great in number, delicate and bulky, short and long, and have different functions. A curious fact about them is that if one muscle functions in a particular direction, another always functions in the opposite direction, and the refinement of the movement depends on this opposition. The individual is not conscious of the opposition, but it is the way movement takes place. To animals perfection of movement is given by nature, and the grace of the tiger or the squirrel is due to a wealth of opposition put into play to attain that harmony. In man this mechanism is not there at birth, so has to be created, and this is done by practical experiments on the environment. It is not so much exercise of movement, but of co-ordination. This co-ordination is not fixed for the human child, but has to be created and perfected through the psyche.

A human characteristic is that he can do all movements, and extend them further than any animal, making some of them his own. He has universal skill in action, but only on one condition, that he first make himself, creating by will at first sub-consciously, and then voluntarily repeating the exercises for co-ordination. Wealthy in potentialities, he chooses which part of his wealth to use. A gymnast is not endowed with a special set of muscles to help him, nor a dancer born with certain refined muscles for his art; both develop them by will. So nothing is established, but everything is possible, under direction of the will; and men do not all do the same things, as animals of a single species. Each man has his own path to follow, and work is a chief expression of his psychic life. Those who do no work are truly in great danger of spiritual atrophy. Though the muscles are too numerous for all to be exercised, there is a certain number below which the psychic life will be endangered. A realization of this has brought about the introduction of gymnastics into education, for too many muscles were being left unused.

The psychic life must use more muscles, but the purpose behind their use should not primarily be utilitarian, as in some forms of modern education called technical. The true aim is that man may develop the co-ordination of movements needed for enriching the practical side of his psychic life. Otherwise the brain must develop a set of movements aside from the central psychic direction, and that brings revolution and disaster in the world. Work may not come first in the art of life, but self-centralization achieved by movement must of necessity expand, and there are no limits to its expansion.

Whereas in all other animals the four limbs develop in movement together, in man alone the function of the legs is quite different from the function of the arms, and they develop differently. It may be noted that the development of walking and equilibrium is fixed in all men, so may be called a biological fact. All men do the same thing with their feet, but not with their hands, of whose activity none knows the limits. Though the function of the feet is biological, it is followed by inner development in the brain, with the result that man walks on two limbs only, while other mammals use four. Once a man has achieved this art of walking on two legs, he keeps the state of erect equilibrium, but it was a difficult achievement – a real conquest, necessitating the placing of the whole foot on the ground, not only the toe as with animals. Evidently the hand has no such biological guidance, since its actions are not fixed, but it has a psychological connection, depending for development not only on the psyche of the individual, but also on the psychic life of different epochs in time, and different racial groups. It is characteristic of man to think and to act with his hands, and from the earliest time he has left traces of his work, rough or fine according to the type of civilization. Looking into the dim past, of which not even bones are left, we gain some knowledge of the people and their times from their works of art; one civilization based on strength which has left behind it colossal masses of stone that excite our wonder, while another is revealed as having had more refinement. The hand has followed the intelligence, spirit and emotions, and has left traces of all behind man in his wanderings. Apart from the psychological point of view, all changes in man's environment have been made by the hand of man. It is because the hands have accompanied the intelligence that civilization has been built, so it may well be said that the hand is the organ of that immense treasure given to man.

Incidentally, the ancient art of palmistry is based on the recognition of the hand as a psychic organ; its practitioners claim that the whole history of the man is written on the palm of his hand. Therefore the study of the psychic development of the child should be closely linked with the study of the development of the hand. Certainly the intelligence of the child will reach a certain level without the use of the hand, but with it a still higher level is reached, and the child who has used his hands invariably has a stronger character. If through force of circumstances he cannot use his hands, the child will have a character of a low type, incapable of obedience or initiative, lazy and sad, whereas the child who can work with his hands shows firmness of character. An interesting point about the Egyptian civilization, during that period when its handiwork was greatest in the fields of art, strength and religion, is that the highest praise given to any man in the inscriptions on tombs was that he was a man of character.

It was made clear in the study of language that speech is connected specially with hearing; similarly the development of movement is found to be connected with sight. The first step in movement is that of grasping or prehension; as soon as the hand grasps something, consciousness is called to the hand, and prehension is developed, that which was at first instinctive becoming a conscious movement. At six months it is fully intentional. At ten months, observation of the environment has awakened the interest of the child, and he wants to catch hold of everything, so prehension is now accompanied by desire. He begins to exercise the hand by changing the places of things around him, by opening and shutting doors, pulling out drawers, putting stoppers in bottles, and so on. Through these exercises, he acquires ability. At this period, with regard to the other limbs neither intelligence nor consciousness has been called forth, though there is rapid development of the cerebellum, the director of equilibrium. The environment has nothing to do with it; the cerebellum orders, and the child, with effort and help, sits up and then gets up by himself. First the baby turns on his stomach and walks on four limbs, and if during this crawling period an adult offers him the help of two fingers to hold, he will make the feet go one in front of the other to stand but on the toes only. When at last he stands by himself, he rests his whole foot on the ground, and can walk by holding on to his mother's skirt; after that he can soon walk alone, and rejoices in this new independence. Now, if the adult continues to help him, it will be an obstacle in his path of development. We must not help the child to walk, and if his hand wants to work, we must give him motives of activity, and leave him to proceed to ever greater conquests of independence.

An important and visible factor at the age of one-and-a-half years is strength in both hands and feet, and, in consequence, the child's urge in doing anything is to use the maximum effort. Equilibrium and the use of the hands have hitherto been developed apart, but now they make contact, and the child likes to walk carrying a load, often quite disproportionate to himself in size. The hand which has learned to grasp must exercise itself by carrying weight. So the child of that age may be seen with a large jug of water, adjusting his equilibrium and walking slowly. There is the tendency also to challenge the law of gravity: not content with walking, he must climb, by grasping something and pulling himself up. Next follows the imitative period, when the child who is free to act will love to do the things that adults around him are doing. So the logic of natural development is seen: first the child prepares his instruments, hands and feet, then he gets strength by exercise, and next looks at what other people are doing, and sets to work in imitation, fitting himself for life and freedom.

At this period of his activity the child is a great walker, in need of long walks, and adults insist on carrying him, or putting him in a perambulator, so the poor child can walk only in imagination. He cannot walk - they carry him; he cannot work – they do it for him! On the threshold of life we adults give him an inferiority complex.

9

IMITATIVE ACTION AND
CYCLES OF ACTIVITY

The age of one-and-a-half years has become a great centre of interest to psychologists, as of the greatest importance in education. Physiologically it is the point at which there is co-ordination between the preparation of upper and lower limbs, and psychologically the child is on the eve of the disclosure of his full manhood, for at two years of age he will complete himself with the explosion of language, and already he is making efforts to give out what is within him.

It is a recognized fact that this is an age of maximum effort, which should be supported, and further that children show an instinct of imitation. People have always said that children were imitative, but it was a superficial statement, requiring that parents and teachers should set a good example for the little ones to follow. The result was not entirely happy, for all thought they must be models of perfection, yet knew themselves to be far from it. We wanted a perfect humanity; we thought that humanity had to become perfect by imitating us; but we were imperfect, so there was a hopeless impasse. But nature has not followed such reasoning. What is important is that the child has to be prepared for imitation, and it is this preparation that matters, depending on the effort of the child. The effort is not in the imitation, but in the creation within the psyche of the possibility of imitation, of transforming oneself into the thing desired. A child cannot become a pianist by mere imitation, but must prepare his hands to gain the necessary agility; and on a loftier level, telling stories of heroes and saints will not make the child heroic or saintly, until his spirit has been prepared. Imitation may furnish inspiration and interest, but there must be a preparation to carry this out. Nature does not merely give

44

the instinct for imitation, but the effort in oneself to become transformed into whatever the example demonstrates; and so those educationists who believe in helping life must see in what ways they can help those efforts.

The child of this age sets out to do a certain task, perhaps an absurd one to adult reasoning, but this matters not at all; he must carry out the activity to its conclusion. There is a vital urge to completeness of action, and if the cycle of this urge is broken, it shows in deviations from normality and lack of purpose. Much importance attaches now to this cycle of activity, which is an indirect preparation for future life. All through life men prepare for the future indirectly, and it is remarked of those who have done something great that there has been a previous period of something worked for, not necessarily on the same line as the final work, but along some line there has been an intense effort which has given the necessary preparation of the spirit, and such effort must be fully expanded – the cycle must be completed. Adults therefore should not interfere to stop any childish activity however absurd, so long as it is not too dangerous to life and limb! The child must carry out his cycle of activity.

This activity takes many interesting forms: one is that of carrying weights far beyond their strength, and for no apparent reason. In the house of a friend I once saw a baby labouring to carry heavy footstools, one by one, from one end of the room to the other. Children of this age will continue carrying things back and forth till they are tired. The adult's usual reaction is to feel pity for the child's weakness, go to help him and take the weight from him; but psychologists have recognized this interruption of a child's chosen cycle of activity to be one of the greatest repressions of this age, leading to difficulties later. Another favourite effort is to climb staircases, but not for the sake of reaching the higher floor, for on getting to the top he must come back to the starting point to complete the cycle. I have seen a child who was climbing a very steep staircase; each step reached to the child's middle, and he had to use both hands to pull himself up, and then put his legs round in a most difficult position; but he had the constancy to reach the top – forty-five steps. Then he looked back to see what he had achieved, overbalanced and fell backward down the stairs. They were thickly carpeted, so did him little injury, and when he had reached the last bump and was at the bottom again, he was left facing us in the room. We thought he would cry, but instead he laughed contentedly as if to say: "How hard to go up and easy to come down!"

Sometimes these efforts are significant of attention and fine co-ordination of movement rather than of strength. One child of one-and-a-half, who was free to wander through the house, came to a linen-room, where twelve large napkins were in a pile, ironed and waiting to be put away. The baby took the top one with both hands, happy to see that it came away from the pile, went along the corridor, and laid it carefully on the floor in the farthest corner. Having done that, he came back for another, and repeated the action for each of the twelve, each time saying to himself "One," as he took it. Having put them all in his chosen place, we thought the action finished, but no! As soon as the last one was in the corner, he started to bring them back to the original place, still carrying them one by one, and saying "One" over each in turn. The attention of the child was marvellous, and he had a delighted expression on his face as he went away, on further business of his own.

At the age of two years the child has a need for walking that most psychologists fail to consider. He can walk for a mile or even two, and if part of it is up-hill, so much the better, for he loves to go up; the difficult points in the walk are the interesting ones. But adults have to realize what walking means to the child; the idea that he cannot walk comes from the fact that they expect him to walk at their rate, and when he cannot, from the shortness of his legs, keep up, they pick him up and carry him to get the quicker to their goal. But the child does not want to get anywhere; he just wants to walk, and to help him truly the adult must follow the child, and not expect him to keep up. The need for following the child is clearly demonstrated here, but indeed it is the rule for all sides of education and in all fields. The child has his own laws of growth, and if we want to help him grow, we must follow him instead of imposing ourselves on him. The child walks with his eyes as well as with his legs, and it is the interesting things on the walk that carry him along. He walks till he sees a lamb feeding; he is attracted and sits by it watching. Satisfied with this experience, he goes further and sees a flower, by which he sits down to sniff it; a little further he is struck by a tree, and walks round it four or five times before going on. In this way he can cover miles; they are full of resting intervals and of interesting discoveries, and if there is something difficult in the way, such as a rock to climb or water to cross, his cup of happiness is full. Water is a main attraction, and sometimes he will sit down and say: "Water," with delight, when the adult would have quite overlooked a tiny stream falling drop by drop. So he has a different idea of walking from that of his nurse, who wants to arrive at a spot in the quickest possible time. She takes him to a park for a walk, or lets him take the air in a perambulator, with the hood up so that he cannot see many things.

Education must consider the walking man, who walks as an explorer; all children should walk in this way, guided by attraction, and here education can help the child by introducing him to the colours, the shapes and forms of leaves, and the habits of insects, animals and birds. All these give point to his interest when he goes out, and the more he learns the more he walks. In itself walking is a complete exercise; there is no need of other gymnastic efforts, for this alone makes the child breathe and digest better than the advantages expected of sports. Beauty of body is built by walking and if the child finds something interesting to pick up and classify, or a trench to dig, or wood to be fetched for a fire, then these actions accompanying walking make the exercise complete.

This must form part of education, especially today, when people seldom walk but go in cars or vehicles of some sort, so that there is a tendency to paralysis and sloth. Life may not be cut in two, moving the limbs by sport, and then the mind by reading. Life must be one whole, especially at an early age, when the child is constructing himself.

It is so difficult to find people who will not interrupt, but will understand and respect the child's independence in following his natural lines of growth, that psychologists ask for places where babies can work, and hence arise schools for very little children, even of one-and-a-half years. All sorts of things are provided in these schools, as houses in trees, with ladders to go up and come down. The tiny house is not to be lived in, but to provide a centre of interest for the climbing activity. It is a recognition that education cannot begin too soon, if we want the man to be a worthy citizen in a free democracy. How can we speak of Democracy or Freedom when from the very beginning of life we mould the child to undergo tyranny, to obey a dictator? How can we expect democracy when we have reared slaves? Real freedom begins at the beginning of life, not at the adult stage. These people who have been diminished in their powers, made short-sighted, devitalized by mental fatigue, whose bodies have become distorted, whose wills have been broken by elders who say: "Your will must disappear and mine prevail!" – how can we expect them, when school-life is finished, to accept and use the rights of freedom?

10

THE THREE-YEAR-OLD

Nature seems to have placed a dividing line between the sub-periods before and after three years. The earlier one, though creative and full of important events, becomes the forgotten period, comparable to the embryonic life before physical birth, for only at three do full consciousness and remembrance begin. In the psychic-embryonic period there were developments which came separately and independently, such as language, movements of limbs and their co-ordination, and certain sensory developments, just as organs were unfolded one by one in the physical embryo before birth; but man remembers nothing of either. This is because there has yet been no unity of personality, such unity coming only with completed parts. This sub-conscious and unconscious creation, this forgotten child, seems to be erased from man, and the child coming to us at three years seems an incomprehensible being; the communication between him and us has been taken away by nature, so either we have to know all that happened in that earlier period, or to know nature herself, lest we unwittingly destroy what she would build. Man has abandoned the natural path of life for the fatal way of civilization, and as civilized humanity has given protection only to the physical and not the psychic part of man, what has resulted for the child is a prison – an environment of obstacles.

The child is entirely in the care of adults, and they, unless enlightened by wisdom of nature or science, will present the greatest obstacles in the child's life. The three-year-old must develop by experimenting on the environment, using what he has created in his earlier years. He has forgotten the events of those years, but the faculties he then created now rise to the surface of consciousness, through experiences carried out consciously.

The hand, guided by the intelligence, does a sort of work, carrying out the psychic will. It is as though the child, who previously has received the world through his intelligence, now takes it in his hands. He wants to perfect his former acquisitions, such as language; it is already complete in its development, but gains enrichment up to four-and-a-half years. The mind still retains the embryonic power of absorbing without fatigue, but it is now the hand which becomes the direct organ of intellectual prehension, and the child develops by working with his hands instead of by walking about. The child at this age is continuously at work; happy and light-hearted if always busy with his hands. Adults call it the blessed age of play, and society has created toys to correspond to the child's activities. Instead of the means to develop his intelligence, he is given useless toys. He wants to touch everything, and they let him touch some things and forbid others; the only real thing they let him touch is sand, and where there is no sand, compassionate man brings it to rich children. Water may also be allowed, but not much of that, because the child gets wet, and water and sand make dirt which adults have to wash! When he tires of sand, they give him small models of things used by adults, miniature kitchens and houses, toy pianos, but such that cannot really be used. They recognize that the child wants to copy them in their work, but they give him in response things with which he cannot work. It is a mockery! To the lonely child they give a mockery of the human figure, a doll, and the doll may become more real to him than father or mother; but dolly cannot answer him or respond to his love, so is an unsatisfactory substitute for society.

The toy has become so important that people think it an aid to the intelligence; it is certainly better than nothing, but it is significant that the child quickly tires of a toy and wants new ones. He wantonly breaks it, and people infer that he has a delight in taking things to pieces and in destruction; but this is an artificially developed characteristic, due to his not having the right things to handle. Children have little interest in these things because there is no reality in them. So they become listless, lacking in attention, and unable to develop normally, till personality is completely deformed. The child at this age seriously and consciously tries to perfect himself by imitation of his elders in all the experiences of life; opportunity being denied him, he must be deformed.

This is especially the tragedy of the highly civilized child; in simpler social circles the child is normally calmer and happier, freely using the objects around him, which are not so precious as to be withheld for fear of accident. If mother washes or bakes bread, the child does it too, if he can find suitable things, and so prepares himself for life.

This fact can no longer be doubted; the child of three must handle things for purposes of his own. When things are made for him in proportion to his size, and he can be active with them just as adults are active, his whole character seems to change, and he becomes calm and contented. He does not care for things that are not in his usual environment, because his work is to suit himself to his own adult world, and nature's purpose is to give joy in the fulfilment of special things. So the new way is to provide motives of activity with objects built suitably to the child's strength and size, and as men usually work at home and on the land, the children must have their own home and their own land. Not toys for children, but houses for them; not toys for them, but land on which they can work with small tools; not dolls for children, but real other children and a social life in which they can act for themselves. These things are our substitutes today for the toys of the past.

Once this barrier was broken, the evil of unreality torn aside and the child given real things, his first reaction was not quite what we had expected. The child showed a different personality, asserting his independence and refusing aid. He surprised mothers, nurses and teachers by showing clearly that he wanted to be left alone, and that they must be mere observers in this environment of which he had become master.

Now with regard to those early experiments of mine, the facts which we were so fortunate as to witness in Rome many years ago would not have happened but for special circumstances. If a House for Children had been organized in a rich quarter of New York, nothing of note would have happened, just as nothing happens in many schools which are richly endowed. It is not lack of objects to handle that alone matters, but other things as well that cause obscuration. The circumstances which favoured the first experiment were mainly three:

EDUCATION FOR A NEW WORLD

1. Extreme poverty and a social condition of much difficulty. The child who is very poor may suffer physically from lack of food, but he finds himself in natural conditions, and so has inner wealth.

2. The parents of these children were illiterate, so could not give them unwise help.

3. The teachers were not professional teachers, so were free from the pedagogic prejudices induced by training on the usual lines. In America experiments never succeeded because they looked for the best teachers, and a good teacher meant one who had studied all the things that do not help the child, and was full of ideas which were opposed to the child's freedom. The imposition of the teacher on the child can only hinder him. One must take simple people, and make use of them, and as to poverty, one need not impose it but must not be frightened of it, as it is a highly spiritual condition. If we want an easy experiment with sure success, we should go to work among poor children, offering them an environment which they do not possess. An object scientifically constructed is received with passionate interest by the child who has had nothing, and it awakens in him mental concentration. Forty years ago this fact caused great surprise, for it had never been seen in children of three years. Yet concentration is a basic act, taking hold of the environment item by item, exploring each one and dwelling on it. Under the usual unsatisfactory conditions, the child flits from one thing to another, concentrating on nothing, but we have proved that such inconstancy is not his real character.

It must be remembered that in the small child of three years the inner teacher is still at work guiding him unerringly, and when we speak of a free child, we mean one following the guidance of that nature which is powerful within him. The child led by nature goes into all the details of a task undertaken, for example, dusting the top, sides, legs, under-surface and even cracks of a table, when only expected to clean the top. Given freedom and no interruptions by the teacher, he devotes full concentrated attention to his work. Too many teachers are inclined to be continually interrupting and teaching, so the child who is developing spontaneously, under nature's guidance, cannot get on with a teacher who teaches. The teacher considers that she must lead him from the easy to the difficult, from simple to complex, by gradual steps, whereas the child may go from the difficult to the easy, and makes great strides. Another prejudice such teachers have is that of fatigue. A child who is interested in what he is doing goes on and on without fatigue, but when the teacher makes him change every few minutes and rest, he loses interest and gets fatigued. But with teachers from the usual types of Training Colleges these prejudices are so deeply rooted that they are incurable. Most modern colleges have this prejudice regarding the need for rest so badly that they have interruptions every three-quarters of an hour, with fatal results. The pedagogical world is guided by human logic, but nature has other laws. Logic distinguishes between mental and physical activities, saying that for mental work we must sit still in class, and for physical work the mental part is not wanted; so it cuts the child in two. When he thinks, he is not allowed to use his hands; but nature shows that the child cannot think without his hands, and that he needs to be continually walking about, like the peripatetic philosophers of Greece. Movement and mind go together yet many think it impossible to have a school where children study, but continually walk about.

The greatest effort in our new method has to be directed towards freeing the teacher from these and other prejudices and the greatest success is the teacher who succeeds in getting free from most of them. So if the education of a great number is envisaged, and there is a scarcity of trained teachers, we can say "Thank God!" It is a favourable condition.

The new teachers must, however, understand certain fundamental things, of little difficulty. For instance, in my first experiment I instructed my assistant, who was the daughter of the porter of the tenements, to present certain objects in a particular fashion and order to the child, and leave him alone with it. Uneducated as she was she was able to do this exactly, and to her surprise, the children worked with those objects to wonderful effect. She thought there were angels or some spirit agencies at work, and would come to me half-frightened to report: "Madame, at two o'clock yesterday this child began to write!" There seemed something supernatural in his writing beautifully formed sentences when he had never written anything in his life before, and could not yet read.

EDUCATION FOR A NEW WORLD

Experience has shown that the teacher must withdraw more and more into the background, only preparing for the children to work by themselves. Our work is to convince the teacher where intervention is needless and even mischievous, and this we call the Method of Non-Intervention. The teacher must measure what is needed, like a servant who prepares with care a drink for his master, and then leaves it for him to drink at will. Teachers have to learn to be humble, not imposing themselves on the children in their care, but ever vigilant to follow their progress, and prepare all that they are likely to need for further activity.

It is the parents of the lower classes who co-operate most heartily with our methods of education. When the child writes his first word – and father and mother cannot write – their adoring wonder at the achievement brings uplift to the child, whereas the richer parents will show little interest, and probably ask the child if they do not teach him art at school, so his achievement seems less important. A child who wants to dust is often told that it is servant's work, and he is not sent to school to learn such menial tasks! Again a mother who finds that her child is learning mathematics at what she considers too tender an age fears brain-fever for him, and wants to stop his work. So the child gets a complex of superiority or inferiority, and is mentally crippled accordingly.

Thus the very conditions thought bad for educational experiment are in reality good, and success does not limit itself to the children, but influences the parents. In my first experimental house, the children who had started doing exercises of practical housekeeping would tell their mothers that they must not have spots on their dresses, and must not spill water, and soon the mothers began to care for clean dresses and order. Parents would want to learn reading and writing because their children knew them, and the whole environment began to be transformed through the children. We seemed to have in our hands a magic wand.

11

METHODS EVOLVED BY

OBSERVATION

It was the explosion into writing that first caught the attention of the public in my early experiment. It was not an explosion merely of writing, but of the human self in the child. A mountain may seem to be solid and eternally unchanged, yet contain an inner fire, which one day erupts through the outer crust. It is an explosion of fire, smoke and unknown substances, which reveal to those who examine them what the interior of the earth is like. Our explosion was the same, and it happened because of circumstances which then seemed the least favourable for such a revelation. Poverty and ignorance, and lack of teachers, syllabus and rules furnished a basic nothing, and because of that nothingness, the soul was able to expand. Obstacles had been unwittingly removed, but none knew at that time what the obstacles were. It was emphatically not any method of education which caused these explosions, because the method did not then exist; psychology followed them up and the method was built as a result of this volcanic eruption in the child. The Press headlined it as the "Discovery of the Human Soul."

The new science that followed was based not on intuition, but on direct perception, and the facts perceived fall into two groups. One shows the mind of the child capable of acquiring culture at an incredibly early age, but only through his own unaided activity; the other deals with the development of character, also at an age that older educators had agreed was too young for influences on character. They were wrong because they thought that it was the adult who had to influence the character of the young; and to turn evil into good is an eternal problem. But the period from three to six is the time for developing character, each child developing by his own laws unless obstructed.

The child concentrates on those things that he already has in his mind, that he has absorbed in the previous period, for whatever has been conquered has a tendency to remain in mind, to be pondered. The explosion into writing was thus due to the previous conquest of speech, and a language sensitivity which ceases at five-and-a-half to six years. Thus only at this age could writing be achieved with such joy and enthusiasm, while children of eight or nine had no such inspiration. It was seen that the children had indirectly prepared the organs for writing, so indirect preparation was adopted as an integral part of the Montessori Method. We had seen that nature prepares indirectly in the embryo; she issues no orders until the organs have been prepared for obedience. Character, can be built only in the same way. Nothing is gained by mere imitation or forced obedience; there must be inner preparation by which obedience becomes possible, and such preparation is indirect. It is essential to prepare the environment for children, and to give them that freedom wherein the soul can expand its powers.

In language development, the child in the earlier period had followed what seemed like a grammatical order in speech, proceeding from sounds and syllables to nouns, adjectives, adverbs, conjunctions, verbs and prepositions. Accordingly we thought it would help him to have a grammatical method in the second period, and our first language teaching was of grammar. It seems absurd, to our usual way of thinking, that grammar should be taught at three, before reading or writing, but the children were keenly interested in it, as older children were not. Grammar after all is the construction of a language, and the child had to construct and found help in it.

The uncultured teachers we had in our schools noted the children's hunger for words, and they wrote for them as many as they knew, and came to me for more, having exhausted their simple vocabulary. We thought we would try the experiment of giving them the words needed for more advanced culture, as the names of geometrical figures, polygons, trapeziums, and others of similar difficulty; the children absorbed them easily in one day. Then we went to scientific instruments, as thermometer and barometer, and to botanical terms, as petals, sepals, stamens and pistil. They were all received with enthusiasm, and we were asked for more, for the age of three to six is one of an insatiable thirst for words, that cannot be too long and complicated for the child. We gave them words used in the various classifications of all subjects – zoology, geography and others – and the only difficulty was with the teachers, who did not know these words, and found it difficult to remember their meanings.

The mind of the child does not limit itself to the objects they can see and their qualities, but goes beyond this, showing imagination. Children for whom a table in play becomes a house, a chair serves as a horse, who can visualize a fairy and fairyland, have no difficulty in visualizing America or the world, especially with a globe to help. Some of our children of six years had a globe, and were talking about it, when a child under four ran up. "Let me see! Is this the world? Now I understand how it is my uncle has gone three times round the world." At the same time he realized that the globe was only a model, for he knew that the world was immense.

A child under five also asked to see one of the globes which were provided for older children. These were talking of America, taking no notice of him, till he interrupted them. "Where is New York?" he asked. They showed him, and the next question was: "Where is Holland?" – that being the country where we then were working. On being shown his own country, the little one touched the blue part of the globe, and said: "Then this is the sea. My father goes to America twice a year and stays in New York. When he has started, Mother tells us, 'Papa is on the sea!' then she says that he is in New York. Now again he is on the sea, and we shall go to meet him soon at Rotterdam." He had heard so much about America, and now he felt joy in discovering it, reaching an orientation in his mental environment just as he formerly had to do in the physical. In order to take the mental world of his time, he has to take words from the elders of his family, and clock them with his own images. This strength of imagination in the child under six is usually expended on toys and fairy tales, but surely we can give him real things to imagine about, so putting him in more accurate relation with his environment.

Another well-known characteristic of children of this age is that they are always asking questions, seeking the truth of things. Such questions should be interesting to the adult, not regarded as a nuisance, but as the expression of a mind seeking information. But children are not able to follow long explanations, and need simple answers, where possible helped by some illustrative object, such as the globe to the child's quest in geography.

The teacher requires a special preparation, because it is not logic that can solve the child's problems. We have to know the child's previous development, and rather to shed our preconceived ideas. Great tact and delicacy are needed for the care of the mind of a child between the ages of three and six; fortunately, the child takes from the environment rather than from the teacher, who needs only to stand by, to serve when called.

Coming now to the important question of character and moral education, here too we were shown that it must be looked at from a different point of view, helping the construction of character, rather than teaching it. For this again the period that ends at six years is the most important, since it is then that character is being formed, not by outside example and pressure, but by nature herself. After birth there are those three important years which we considered earlier, during which there are influences that can alter the child's character for life. A character is being created even then, from obstacles or in freedom from them. If during conception, gestation, birth and the subsequent period the child has had scientific care, then at the age of three the child should be a model individual; but this seldom happens, for the child has usually met with many accidents.

If defects of character are due to difficulties after birth, they are less serious than those induced in the time of gestation, and those in turn are less serious than those of conception. If they are post-natal, defects can be cured between three and six years, as this is the time for adjustment and the attainment of perfection. But mental and physical defects due to the shock of birth, or to some earlier cause, are very difficult to correct. Idiocy, epilepsy and paralysis are organic, and cannot be cured by any help that we can give; but difficulties that are not organic can be cured, if treated before the age of six; otherwise they will not only remain, but will grow and be strengthened. A child of six years is likely to be an accumulation of characteristics that are not really his, but acquired through his experiences. A child who has been neglected from three to six is unlikely to have the moral conscience that should develop from seven to twelve, or he may be deficient in intelligence. With no moral character and no ability to learn, he becomes a man of scars, marks of past defeats of the soul.

In our schools, and in many other modern ones, we have biological details of each child, so that we may know the troubles of different periods, and judge their treatment accordingly. We ask if there is any hereditary illness; the parents' age when the child was born; whether the mother was free from accidents or nervous shocks during the gestation period, whether the birth has been normal and the baby well, or did it suffer from asphyxia. Enquiries into the home life follow, if parents or nurses have been severe, or the child has had any shock. This questionnaire is necessary because almost all children come to us with strange characteristics and naughtinesses, and these must be traced and understood in order to be cured.

All these deviations from the normal enter almost at once into the field of what most people, rather vaguely, call character, and they fall into two groups: the strong children who overcome obstacles, and the weak ones who succumb to them. The strong children show readiness to anger, acts of rebellion, destructiveness, greed for possession and selfishness, inattention and disorderliness of mind and imagination. These children often shout and are noisy, like to tease and are cruel to animals. Frequently they are greedy. The weak children are passive and show negative defects, such as sloth, inertia, crying for things, and wanting everything to be done for them. They have a fear of everthing strange, and cling to adults. They want always to be amused, and are quickly bored and tired; they have the faults of lying and of stealing, fundamentally forms of self-defence.

Certain physical ailments go with these difficulties, and thus show a psychic origin that should not be confused with real physical sickness. Such is want of appetite, or its opposite – gluttony – and indigestion due to it. Liability to nightmares and fear of the dark affect the physical health and cause anaemia. No medicine can cure them as their origin is psychic.

Children who have these faults, especially of the strong type, are not felt as blessings in their family; they are banished to the nursery or to the school, and they are orphans though their parents are living.

Some parents adopt severity, such as slapping, scolding, sending to bed without food, but the children either become worse or develop the passive equivalent of the difficulty. Then they try the persuasive line, reasoning with them and exploiting their affection: "Why do you hurt Mummy?" It has no effect. The parents of the passive type of regressed children are apt to leave them doing nothing, the mother thinking her boy good and obedient, and when he clings to her and won't go to sleep without her at his side, she thinks it a sign only of his great affection for her. But soon she finds that he is slow and retarded in speech and walking. Though healthy, he is afraid of everything and doesn't want to eat, needing stories to coax him. She persuades herself that he is a spiritual child, perhaps destined to be a saint or a poet, but soon the doctor is called to give him medicine. These psychic illnesses make a fortune for the family doctor.

One of the facts that made our first schools remarkable was the disappearance of these defects, and it was due to one thing. The children could freely carry out their experiments on the environment, and these experiences were nourishment to the mind, which had been starved. Once some interest had been aroused, they repeated exercises around that interest, and passed from one concentration to another. When the child has reached the stage of being able to concentrate and work round an interest, the defects disappear; the disorderly become orderly, the passive active and the disturber becomes a helper; thus the defects are revealed as not real but acquired characteristics. So our advice to mothers is to give the children work in some interesting occupation, and never interrupt them in any action they have started. Sweetness, severity, medicine do not help at all. We do not sentimentalize over the troublesome child, or call him stupid; that would do no good when he is needing mental food. Man is by nature an intellectual being, and needs mental food even more than physical. Unlike the animals, he must construct his own behaviour from life and its experiences, and if set on this road of life, all will be well.

12

THE BUGBEAR OF DISCIPLINE

It has been established that moral education means only the development of character, and that faults can be made to disappear without the need of preaching, punishment or even setting a good example by the adult. Neither threats nor promises are needed, but conditions of life.

In addition to the so-called good (or passive) and the naughty types that have already been considered, the world generally recognizes a third type of child, who is extremely healthy, has a vivid imagination, turns from one thing to the other, and is regarded as specially bright by parents – in fact superior! What I have seen in my schools is that those characteristics all disappeared as soon as the child became interested in work that attracted his attention. The so-called good and bad and superior alike merged into one type of child with none of these traits at all. This shows that the world has not hitherto been able to measure good and evil, and was wrong in its judgment. The real aim of all children was revealed as constancy in work and spontaneity in choice of work, without guidance of teachers. Following some inner guide, they occupied themselves in work different for each that gave them joy and peace, and then something else appeared that had never before been known among children, a spontaneous discipline. This struck visitors even more than the explosion into writing had done; children were walking about, seeking work in freedom, each concentrating on a different task, yet the whole group presented the appearance of perfect discipline. So the problem was solved: to obtain discipline, give freedom. It is not necessary for the adult to be a guide or mentor in conduct, but to give the child opportunities of work that have been hitherto denied.

It seemed at first impossible that a group of forty children could be in one room, working quietly without the guidance of a teacher, especially since they were aged from three to five years. The newspapers declared it marvellous if true, but incredible! Visitors tried to find out what trick I used, for they were sure it was a trick. Some said it was my personal magnetism or hypnotism that produced the result, but I was able to say: "This happened in New York, when I was in Rome!" for it was no sporadic phenomenon, but was happening in all our schools, which had spread to America, New Zealand, France and England. Other sceptics concluded that the children had been prepared for visitors by the teacher, or that she used her eyes in some way to express approval or disapproval. But evidence accumulated from all countries; a common factor was the extraordinary discipline of the "normalized" children, as we called the type that developed in our schools, as compared with "deviated" children.

In my first Children's House, all the children came from the same tenement house. Among other unbelievers was the ambassador of the Argentine Republic, who happened to be in Rome. He wanted to see the school for himself, and to go without previous notice, so that no preparations could be made for the visit. He told his intention to the daughter of the Prime Minister of Italy, who promised to accompany him, and to give no warning to the school. They had forgotten that it was Thursday, a holiday in Italian primary schools, so the school was closed; but a small child came up to them, to ask if they wanted anything. He was only four years old, and poor children of this age do not usually talk freely with rich strangers; but he was quite natural in his manner, and, when told that they had wanted to see the school and regretted that it was closed, he said: "Oh, that doesn't matter! The porter has the key, and all the children live here, so I can call them." To the visitors' amazement, the children all came very willing, and worked with zest and complete absence of disorder though the teacher was not present. The ambassador declared no case could ever have been more conclusively proved, and he became a firm believer in the method.

Another such occasion arose at the World Fair in San Francisco, at the time of the opening of the Panama Canal.

THE BUGBEAR OF DISCIPLINE

Among educational exhibits there was a small Montessori class-room, with glass walls so that people could look on from outside, without disturbing the children by entry. Helen Parkhurst was the teacher, and the room was locked at night, a caretaker taking the key. One day this caretaker did not turn up, having had an accident; people waited outside, as also the children and their teacher. Miss Parkhurst at last said, "We cannot get in to work today"; but one of the children saw an open window, and said, "Lift us up, and we will get through the window and work." The window was of a size proportionate to that of the children, and Miss Parkhurst said, "That is all right for you, but I cannot get through that window!" "No matter," was the answer: "You don't work anyhow. You can sit outside and watch with the other people." So the difficulty was surmounted, and the method scored an unexpected victory.

Only after six years can children benefit from moral teaching, for between six and twelve years of age the conscience awakes, and the child becomes interested in problems of right and wrong. Still more success is possible between twelve and eighteen, when ideals of religion and patriotism are felt.

The main preoccupations concerning character-training are with will and obedience, and the usual aim is to curb the will of the child, substituting the teacher's will for his, and demanding of him obedience. There is great confusion in these topics, which need clarification. Biological studies tell us that the will of man is part of the universal power called Horme, and this is no physical force, but a cosmic energy of life on the path of evolution. Evolution is governed by laws, and is far from being haphazard or casual. As an expression of this force, the will of man has to shape his behaviour, and becomes partly conscious in the child as soon as he has a certain action to carry out, so only through experience. In being natural he obeys law.

It is a mistake to think that the voluntary actions of children are disorderly and sometimes violent; such actions are not expressions of the will of the child, for they are outside the field of horme. It is as if we mistook the contortions of a man in convulsions for acts dictated by his will. If we consider all disorderly movements in child or man as directed by will, it is natural to feel that such will must be curbed or broken, and he must be made obedient. A great educator has said, "The essence of education can be included in one word – obedience." Human logic would persuade that by making a child obedient, he can be taught all the virtues, and them must perforce be virtuous! But on those lines it would seem that the fundamental vice of the child is "disobedience," and the problem is far from being solved.

Happily the problem is not insoluble! The will of man is not expressed in disorder or violence; that is the mark of suffering – of violation! But whereas the breaking of the will is instantaneous, the development of it is a lengthy process, because it is growth, and depends on aid from the environment.

This long process of developing the will may be compared to the spinning of thread; developed by activity in an ever-widening field of action, the thread of will becomes stronger and stronger. By associating these activities with a central aim, as in laying a table or serving food, the children's free wills can be directed continuously to the same purpose, and we get a society by cohesion through will, more even than a society by cohesion through sympathy. Emotion is not paramount here, but will be the cohesive force, and as all want – or will – the same thing, an association comes of calm behaviour that is marvellous to see. But the will must first have been developed in each child.

A surprising event that took place in my first school brought a new practical contribution to the method of education in the form of the Silence Lesson. I went into a class that was seriously at work; the children already had developed wills. I entered this class of forty-five children with an infant of four months in my arms. It was an old Italian custom to swathe the baby's legs tightly round with cloth, so that these were perforce quite still and fixed, and showing my burden to the children I said, "Here is a visitor! See how still he is; I am sure you could not keep so still!" I had thought that they would laugh at my joke, but all became very serious, and at once put their feet together and refrained from movement. Thinking they had not understood my meaning, I went on, "If only you could feel how gently he breathes; you could not breathe so gently, because your chests are bigger." Now I thought they would laugh but not at all. They kept their feet quite still, and even controlled their breath to make it noiseless, and all looked seriously at me. I then said, "I will walk out very quietly, but the baby will be quieter than I; he will not move or make any noise." I took the tiny one back to the mother, and returned to the children, to find them still motionless, and with a look on their faces that said, "See, you made a little noise, but we can be just as quiet as that baby." So all the children had the same will; all were urged to do the same thing, and the result was a class of forty-five perfectly still and silent. People would have wondered how such a wonderful discipline had been achieved, and it had been my intention only to make the children laugh. The silence was so striking that I said, "What a silence!" – and the children seemed also to feel its quality, and remained still, controlling their breath, till I began to hear sounds that I had not noticed before, such as the ticking of the clock, water dripping from an outside tap, and the buzzing of flies. This silence was a cause of great joy to the children, and from it developed a feature of our schools. By it could be measured the strength of will of the children, and with its exercise the will became stronger and the silence period lengthened. Soon we added the whispering of the name of each child, and at the whispered call he came noiselessly, while the others remained quiet and since each came carefully and slowly in their effort to make no sound, the last child to be called had a long time to wait. These children showed themselves capable of far greater inhibitory power than most adults, and it is will and inhibition that give obedience.

I had unintentionally stimulated this first silence by bringing in the baby, but I could not always depend on such a visitor, and wanted to repeat the interest. I found that the best way was to ask, "Would you like to make silence?" Immediately there was great enthusiasm, and I found that I could command silence, and be obeyed. The experience of a teacher who had already taught some ten years is interesting in this connection. She found that she had to check herself from giving directions in advance,such as "Put everything away before going home tonight," because the children began to act before her sentence was finished and its meaning clear. Similar things began to happen with every command, and she felt very responsible when she spoke, because of this immediate reaction. Truly obedience is the last phase of the developed will, so the development of the will alone makes obedience possible, and the good teacher learns scrupulously to avoid taking advantage of the obedience of the children. It is responsibility that a leader should feel, not the authority of his position. After seven the children will seek such a leader; before that age they have social cohesion.

The growth of obedience can be traced in three steps:

1.   The physiological ability to do the task. Till this is developed the child may obey today, but refuse tomorrow, not from any will, but lack of complete development of this stage.

2.   Capacity always to obey, automatically.

3.   The highest form of obedience – very rare in adults – shown in being anxious, eager and happy to obey.

If a child carries out the will of a teacher because he is afraid, or because his affection is exploited, he has no will, and obedience that is secured by suppression of the will is truly oppression. Such is often the obedience obtained in schools, but the finesse of discipline is to obtain obedience from developed wills, and this is based on a society by cohesion, the first step to organized society.

The social cohesion may be compared to the warp of a material, the threads of the personality arranged side by side and fixed to something to keep them orderly. In our case, the environment is what fixes the children's threads, and after six years another thread begins to close together these separate threads, weaving in and out to organize them. Once they are woven together they no longer need support. So we get an insight into the natural course of social embryology. It is usual to regard society as based on government and laws; the children reveal that there must first be individuals of developed will, and then a call which brings them together preceding organization. First strength of will is needed, then cohesion by sentiment, and last cohesion by will.

13

WHAT A MONTESSORI

TEACHER NEEDS TO BE

A superficial judgment of the Montessori Method is too often that it requires little of the teacher, who has to refrain from interference and leave the children to their own activity. But when the didactic material is considered, its quantity and the order and details of its presentation, the task of the teacher becomes both active and complex. It is not that the Montessori teacher is inactive where the usual teacher is active; rather all the activities we have described are due to active preparation and guidance of the teacher, and her later "inactivity" is a sign of her success, representing the task successfully accomplished. Blessed are the teachers who have brought their class to the stage where they can say, "Whether I am present or not, the class carries on. The group has achieved independence." To arrive at this mark of success, there is a path to follow for the teacher's development.

An ordinary teacher cannot be transformed into a Montessori teacher, but must be created anew, having rid herself of pedagogical prejudices. The first step is self-preparation of the imagination, for the Montessori teacher has to visualize a child who is not yet there, materially speaking, and must have faith in the child who will reveal himself through work. The different types of deviated children do not shake the faith of this teacher, who sees a different type of child in the spiritual field, and looks confidently for this self to show when attracted by work that interests. She waits for the children to show signs of concentration.

In this work there are three stages of development:

1. As guardian and custodian of the environment the teacher concentrates on this, instead of being preoccupied by

the difficulties of the problem child, knowing that the cure will come from the environment. Here lies the attraction that will polarize the will of the child. The didactic material must be always beautiful, shining and in good repair, with nothing missing, so that it looks new to the child, and is complete and ready for use. The teacher, as part of the environment, must herself be attractive, preferably young and beautiful, charmingly dressed, scented with cleanliness, happy and graciously dignified. This is the ideal, and cannot always be perfectly reached, but the teacher who presents herself to the children should remember that they are great people, to whom she owes understanding and respect. She should study her movements, making them as gentle and graceful as possible, so that the child may unconsciously pay her the compliment of thinking her as beautiful as his mother, who is naturally his ideal of beauty.

2. In the second stage the teacher has to deal with the children who are still disorderly, with those aimlessly wandering minds which have to be attracted to concentration on some work. The teacher needs to be seductive, and can use any device – except of course the stick – to win the children's attention. She can do what she likes more or less, because as yet she upsets by her intervention nothing very important, so a bright manner in suggesting activities is the chief necessity. Children who persist in molesting others must be stopped for such activity need not be brought to completion.

3. Once the children's interest has been aroused, usually by some exercise of practical life for the material has not yet suitable conditions for its presentation, the teacher withdraws into the background, and must be very careful not to interfere – absolutely not, in any way. Mistakes are often made here, as for instance by uttering an encouraging "Good," in passing a hitherto naughty child, who at last is concentrating on some work. Such well-meant praise is enough to do damage; the child will not look at work again for weeks. Again, if the child is in some difficulty, the teacher must not show him how to get over it, or the child loses interest, for the point to him is conquest of that difficulty not the task in itself. A child who is lifting something too heavy for him does not want help; even for him to see the teacher looking at him is often enough to stop him working. As soon as concentration appears, the teacher should

pay no attention, as if that child did not exist. At least, he must be quite unaware of the teacher's attention. Even if two children want the same material, they should be left to settle the problem for themselves unless they call for the teacher's aid. Her duty is only to present new material as the child exhausts the possibilities of the old. The child who has done some concentrated work may choose to show it to the teacher, to get approbation, and then he should have it ungrudgingly and sincerely: "How beautiful!" The teacher rejoices with the child over the flower of accomplishment.

Montessori teachers are not servants of the child's body, to wash, dress and feed him – they know that he needs to do these things for himself in developing independence. We must help the child to act for himself, will for himself, think for himself; this is the art of those who aspire to serve the spirit. It is the teacher's joy to welcome the manifestations of the spirit, answering her faith. Here is the child as he should be: the worker who never tires, the calm child who seeks the maximum of effort, who tries to help the weak while knowing how to respect the independence of others, in reality, the true child.

Our teachers thus penetrate the secret of childhood, and have a knowledge far superior to that of the ordinary teacher who becomes acquainted only with the superficial facts of the children's lives. Knowing the child's secret, she had a deep love for him, perhaps for the first time understanding what love really is. It is on a different level from the personal love that is shown by caresses, and the difference has been brought about by the children, who by their revelations of spirit have profoundly moved their teacher, bringing her to a level of which she had not known the existence; now she is there and she is happy. Her happiness before was perhaps to draw as high a salary as she could get, and do as little as she need for it; some satisfaction there was for her in her exercise of power and influence, and her hope was to become a headmistress or an inspectress. But there is no real happiness in this, and one would readily leave it all to feel the greater spiritual happiness which the child can give, for "Of such is the Kingdom of Heaven."